# Veganism in an Oppressive World

D1166812

## JULIA FELIZ BRUECK

A Vegans-of-Color Community Project

## Sanctuary Publishers

**Copyright © 2017 by Sanctuary Publishers**

**All rights reserved.**

This book may not be reproduced, in whole or in part, in any form without written permission from the publisher.

**ISBN-13: 978-0-9989946-1-1**

Sanctuary Publishers, www.sanctuarypublishers.com

-A Book Publisher That Gives Back-

Every book sold supports marginalized communities.

# DEDICATION

To all oppressed peoples – human and nonhuman.

May humans embrace the path that leads to justice for *all*.

# CONTENTS

# ACKNOWLEDGMENTS

Thank you to each contributing author – I've learned so much from each of you. Your words have widened my own perception of the world.

Thank you especially to Margaret Robinson for your scholar explanations of intersectionality and to Saryta Rodríguez for your on-point note to vegan organizations – it's an honor to raise your voices of knowledge.

Also, a warm thank you to artist Meneka Repka and graphic designer Danae Silva Montiel – your artistic abilities are an inspiration. I could not have imaged a more wonderful and fitting cover for this community project.

Last but not least, thank you to the organization Deutscher Jugendschutz-Verband for your kind support, which helped make this project come to life.

Thank you all for believing in this book and for lending your unique voices to speak on behalf of justice for *all*.

I'm truly grateful for each and every one of you – this project would not exist without you.

To the reader, thank you for being open to our message and for implementing the changes needed to help veganism achieve a higher level of justice through awareness and action.

# PREFACE

Recent events in the political and social realms have reawakened (and, in some cases, awakened for the first time) people across the world to the injustices towards both human and nonhuman animals that pervade societies worldwide. Billions of animals— human and nonhuman alike— are exploited, abused and murdered each and every year. Climate change denial persists, despite environmental extremes affecting people, wildlife, and natural areas globally, and both social media and independent news sources have shone a spotlight on justice issues, such as the racial inequalities that afflict black and brown bodies every day.

How does this all relate to veganism? As Audre Lorde once said, "we do not live single-issue lives." All social justice movements are interconnected because we humans exist within a system that relies on inequality. As vegans of color, we fight for nonhuman animal rights, yet we also have to fight for our own rights in a world based on white supremacy and systemic oppression.

Through this book, we, myself and contributors from various communities of color, will give you the tools with which to better understand what it means to be a vegan of color and the importance of ensuring that the vegan movement becomes one that opposes *all* oppression. With this vital knowledge and awareness, you will be able to help veganism spread beyond what is perceived as a privileged, mostly-white centered community. People of color make up the largest percent of people on Earth, and, without us— without taking our struggles seriously, and without being mindful of our voices— humans will never be able to create a world in which nonhumans are free from exploitation, which is what unites us in our commitment under veganism.

In preparation to help you on your journey, my goal is not to reinvent the wheel. It is to raise as many voices as possible from vegans of color who have been guiding and continue to guide the vegan movement in a direction that is mindful of various human communities and united against all oppression. You will find a variety of voices quoted throughout the introduction, which will then lead you to individual vegan voices of color. I implore you to learn more about the writings from those quoted and the work that they put forth across different movements as they relate to veganism and nonhuman animal rights. I have also attempted to gather the voices from as many communities that wanted to share their story with you, the reader. Because I was not able to include all communities, I do want to remind you to use this book as a stepping-stone rather than an endpoint in your journey towards ethical consistency: promoting and developing a just society in which veganism extends beyond how you see the world through your own eyes and experiences into the realm of how all living beings are treated and the level of autonomy they are granted.


Julia Feliz Brueck

# 1 INTRODUCTION

If you are skeptical about embracing a consistent anti-oppression and pro-intersectional approach in your veganism, or simply want to learn more about what it means to embrace a movement that is truly just in its fight for nonhumans, then this is a pretty good place to start.

This book is a community-led project by vegans of color in an attempt to use our own voices to raise those of nonhuman animals. Through personal stories, unique lenses, and research-based essays, we hope to give you a sense of why inclusivity of anti-oppression in discussing and campaigning around veganism is imperative for growing our movement in a way that benefits humans and nonhumans alike. With this body of work, we are advocating for our own movement to embrace an approach to veganism: one that is anti-speciesist, consistent, pro-intersectional, and against all oppression.

**Veganism and Anti-Speciesism**

Every word has a beginning, and while people have a tendency to transform the meanings of words as conversations deepen and movements evolve, it is important that some words remain rooted in their humble beginnings. That is the case for the word "vegan."

The term "vegan" was coined in 1945 by Donald Watson and Dorothy Morgan of The Vegan Society, UK. Currently, the Vegan Society defines veganism as, "*a way of living that seeks to exclude, as far as possible and practicable, all forms of exploitation of, and cruelty to, animals for food, clothing, and any other purpose.*" Despite specifically addressing the forms in which humans oppress nonhumans, it is a common claim in vegan circles that the term "veganism" extends beyond nonhumans to include human issues because humans are animals as well. However, while it is true that humans are biologically classified as part of the animal kingdom, it is important to keep in mind that veganism is a movement specifically created to oppose the injustices forced on nonhuman animals *by* humans. This means that, in a relationship where humans are the oppressors and other animals are the oppressed, humans should not be at the center of a movement created to address the oppression of nonhuman animals. To uphold speciesism in the animal rights movement would mean to uphold human supremacy, an ideology in which human needs are consistently placed above those of nonhumans, thus replicating the same oppressor/oppressed relationship against which our movement stands.

In order to clearly outline the Oppressor versus Oppressed relationship of humans and nonhumans that the vegan/animal rights movement attempts to disrupt, veganism should always be referred to as an ethical position against nonhuman animal exploitation. As a political movement that seeks justice for an oppressed group, veganism must define the specific guidelines that will aid humans in achieving liberation for nonhuman animals from human animal exploitation, "*as is possible and practicable*". This does not mean that veganism should not evolve in itself as different communities of vegans learn how to apply anti-oppression of nonhuman animals according to their own cultures and how they experience veganism independently of others. As Syl and Aph Ko explained in their book *Aphro-ism* (2017), human identities affect how we perceive and react to issues with which we are confronted. This means that the practice of veganism will and does change depending on someone's lived experiences and cultural background.

We live in a very non-vegan world, where those who embrace veganism need to make choices against animal exploitation *when possible*— when there are alternatives available. Currently, this is often not the case with items and processes such as medicines, medical procedures, how our plant foods may be grown, etc.

To recognize that vegans are actually the oppressors in the human-nonhuman relationship, and accepting that veganism is neither "cruelty-free" by default nor a lifestyle that can be carried out to perfection, is to acknowledge that vegans themselves are inherently speciesist. Despite this, as a movement and individually, vegans can work collectively to be as anti-speciesist as possible through speech, advocacy, behavior, and other means.

As a basis, vegans must:

- ✓ **...uphold the reason for veganism**, which is a stance against nonhuman animal exploitation and centers nonhumans in their own movement. Vegans must reject the idea that veganism upholds human rights by default— that just by going vegan, one immediately stops partaking in human oppression or exploitation. As a movement centered on fighting nonhuman oppression, veganism does not automatically mean "free from all oppression." *In its current form, mainstream veganism and animal rights are not free from human exploitation and at times, openly excuse and take part in the oppression of marginalized human groups.* For example, nonhuman animal-free products made from plants picked by exploited field laborers or through child labor, clothes made by exploited factory workers, and many more products that we use and even depend on would not be commonly accepted as "vegan" if human rights were also automatically part of veganism. Animal rights and veganism are merely part of the social justice framework needed to work towards a just society, but currently, they are not automatically all encompassing against all oppression. While nonhuman animal oppression and human oppression can be interlinked, some issues that affect humans rights are unrelated to nonhuman oppression. Vegans need to be conscious of supporting a veganism that centers nonhumans without further oppressing humans.

Moreover, the health and environmental benefits of veganism should not take center stage as reasons for "going vegan." When we focus on health or the environment, we put human needs above those of nonhuman animals and again decenter nonhumans from their own movement. That's not to say that the very real benefits of veganism do not merit any mention. They do, especially in current times when society faces threats related to climate change, as well as the knowledge that for *some,* plant-based diets may help reverse diseases. However, when speaking about veganism, the reason behind the concept (nonhumans) should not be minimized in a movement specifically set up to highlight the injustices of nonhuman animal exploitation.

✓ **...reject single-issue advocacy.** In their peer-reviewed essay, published within the *Food, Culture, & Society Journal*, C. L. Wrenn & R. Johnson (2013) explained that single-issue campaigns are speciesist because they focus on one form of exploitation at a time, based on a system in which humans— the oppressors— decide the worth of various species of animal and award privileges to some, but not others. Often, this is done through the assumption that species of lower favoritism to humans would be more difficult to liberate, while it would be easier to convince people to stop exploiting members of species that rank higher in the hierarchy of human favoritism. This, unfortunately, leads to the silencing of the most marginalized species, which includes those considered vermin, as well fish and invertebrates, like insects.

Sadly, it is not uncommon to find so-called vegans advocating for the exploitation of a few "less-developed" species. Wrenn further noted that less favored species will sometimes become victim to reform campaigns because activists hold the belief that nonvegans will never truly support their full liberation. In essence, we have the oppressing class deciding which species deserve attention and which do not. In taking this approach, our movement fails to protect the entirety of the very oppressed group for which we claim our movement *is*.

✓ **...recognize that the way in which we speak about veganism matters.** Veganism is not a diet. Interchanging *vegan* with *plant-based* is speciesist, as it focuses on "food animals" while ignoring those used for clothing, entertainment, testing, and all other forms of exploitation. It also equates plant-based products produced via exploitative labor practices with those produced in most just ways. This further reduces our movement to one that only exists for *some* species.

✓ **...be consistent in their advocacy against animal exploitation.** Allowing for "a little" oppression and advocating for "baby steps" or "reductionism" instead of veganism is speciesist. This does not mean that we should not support those that are seeking to embrace veganism and working towards veganism, but who haven't achieved it yet. It means that we must speak of veganism as the moral goal one should strive for on behalf of nonhuman animals in order to achieve animal liberation from human exploitation. Encouraging people to "reduce" animal products once a week or to give up certain animal foods before others can backfire and may even prevent people from embracing veganism as they find this "middle ground" an easier and more convenient space to occupy.


## Veganism and Anti-Oppression

Upholding an anti-speciesist approach does not mean perpetuating human oppression. On the contrary, vegans must recognize that if we are going to win the fight for nonhuman animal liberation, we must also openly join the fight against human oppression.

Individual choices in embracing a vegan lifestyle depend greatly on accessibility, since access is not the same for all humans due to the different types of oppressions groups of people experience themselves. *Access* has to do with more than mere *affordability*. History and culture also influence the relationship that certain communities have with nonhumans. Climate, mental health, and legal issues can also play a role. Therefore, understanding and truly accepting the practicability portion of the definition and how different oppressions impact the choices of every individual based on their own oppression ties into the need for the vegan movement to embrace an approach that is intersectional, consistently anti-oppression, and understanding of all communities.

Civil rights activist Kimberlé Crenshaw (2015) explained that intersectionality, a term she coined, is *"...a way of thinking about identity and its relationship to power. Originally articulated on behalf of black women, the term brought to light the invisibility of many constituents within groups that claim them as members, but often fail to represent them. Intersectional erasures are not exclusive to black women. People of color within LGBTQ movements; girls of color in the fight against the school-to-prison pipeline; women within immigration movements; trans women within feminist movements; and people with disabilities fighting police abuse — all face vulnerabilities that reflect the intersections of racism, sexism, class oppression, transphobia, able-ism and more. Intersectionality has given many advocates a way to frame their circumstances and to fight for their visibility and inclusion."* Although the concept of intersectionality was not developed specifically with veganism in mind, it is useful in helping to explain how veganism is a privileged movement in its current state and how speciesism can work hand-in-hand with other forms of oppression against marginalized communities.

Indigenous vegan and academic Margaret Robinson (2017) explained that intersectionality is further "helpful for understanding how experiences of advantage and disadvantage are shaped by systems of privilege and oppression related to racialization, ability, gender, sexuality, class, and other categories." Robinson used herself as an example; she is "disadvantaged as an Indigenous woman while also receiving privilege when read by others as White."

She added, "Similarly, the way that I am oppressed as a bisexual person is specific to being a woman, since bisexual men's oppression is different...Another contribution of intersectionality theory is the insight that identities cannot be compartmentalized. Lisa Bowleg's 2008 article, 'When Black+ lesbian+ woman≠ Black lesbian woman,' highlights that identities are not additive—that is, the experience of being a black lesbian woman cannot be measured by adding up the impacts of racism, homophobia, and sexism."

Through this concept, Robinson clarified that she is "never only a woman or only a vegan, a bisexual, or a Mi'kmaq; rather, [her] identities are 'intersecting, interdependent, and mutually constitutive' (Bowleg 2008)."

Robinson further highlighted that in 1983, "Audre Lorde wrote that "[r]acism and homophobia are real conditions of all our lives" Lorde emphasizes that all lives are shaped by white supremacy (the elevation of one category of people-deemed White-above all others), and heteronormativity (the framing of attraction between binary sexes as superior to all other forms of attraction). This includes the lives of those marked as straight and White. By extension, speciesism impacts the lives of human animals as well, creating a hierarchy among us based on our assumed similarity to or distance from other animals."

Robinson found this is "reflected in the way Indigenous people are treated as if we are more like other animals than Settlers [non-Indigenous people] are and therefore, ill-equipped to make good decisions about, our territories, our bodies, or our lives..." Incredulously, Indigenous people were historically classified "as part of the flora and fauna, enabling Settlers to justify treating us as a natural resource to be used, controlled, and managed instead of as people with a claim to the land on which we had lived (Gorman, 2016). This was the case with the Indigenous peoples of Australia, who were literally classified as part of the flora and fauna until the 1967 national referendum amended their Constitution (Marks, 2013)."

Speciesism and racism have traditionally worked hand-in-hand to perpetuate "the notion that minorities are not just inferior to the majority...but that they are as inferior as animals; ergo animals are also inferior to the majority..." which justifies the idea "that while minorities are themselves animals, members of the majority are not... (Rodríguez 2015)."

Robinson further explained that, "intersectionality theory also highlights the connection between speciesism and sexism, revealing the way that female animals and feminized others, including the land, are treated as objects for domination and rape (Adams, 1990). Given the ongoing problem of missing and murdered Indigenous women in Canada, the US, and elsewhere, it is important to highlight the role that the intersection of sexism and speciesism play in making it possible for individuals, the general public, police agencies, and governments to treat Indigenous women as if our suffering is unreal, or unimportant."

Systemic oppression, enforced by society and its institutions, is something that marginalized communities, including vegans of color, must navigate every single day of their lives. Skin color, gender, and race are just a few determinants of the types of oppression someone one will face. As it stands, the vegan movement is centered on a majority of vegans from a group that does not have to navigate through life with these intersecting oppressions. Unfortunately, the refusal of the vegan majority to acknowledge how these oppressions work and how they affect other communities continues to sustain nonhuman oppression and in turn, inaccessibility of the vegan movement itself.

Within communities of color, veganism has garnered an image of being a movement solely for privileged white communities, untouched by the realities that affect marginalized peoples, especially while loudly proclaiming that veganism is "easy;" that nonhuman animal lives are of more importance than oppressed humans ("Nonhuman animals first!"); and that anyone who doesn't adopt a vegan lifestyle simply "doesn't care." The reality is that the mainstream vegan movement is currently oppressive in nature and unwilling to take into account the very real struggles and racialized history that keep whole communities of people from embracing a lifestyle that is easily attainable to communities that don't struggle with the bare necessities and accessibility as the standard. Easy access to grocery stores, farmer's markets, and other venues that offer fresh foods is just one of those privileges not always afforded to many people of color in the U.S. Dr. Breeze Harper from *Sistah Vegan Project* writes, "The awareness just isn't there in many vegan circles and in the country at large that many Americans have little access to affordable, wholesome, plant-based foods. Cheetos, sugar cereals and ramen noodles – YES. Fresh produce or even an affordable can of...beans – NO. (2016)"

In "Here's Why Black People Don't Go Vegan," Nzinga Young (2016) illuminated that communities of color are more likely to live in areas designated as "food deserts," which means accessibility to fresh produce is not a possibility for many. In addition, culturally, "centuries of enslavement and poverty means making do with what you have...when meat is seen as a cultural connection and a means of survival, it'll take time for the black community to see "normal" meals in a negative light." This is just part of the puzzle of dealing with life in an oppressive society for centuries.

In an essay titled, "Food-Systems-Racism: From Mistreatment to Transformation," which appeared in the Winter-Spring issue of *Food First*, Dr. Breeze Harper & Eric Holt-Gímenez (2016) delineated how the racial caste system in the USA, borne out of a history of social, religious, and grossly misinformed biological claims that ensured those not labeled "Caucasian" were seen as inferior, has shaped the food system. This food system is one that is "unjust and unsustainable but it is not broken—it functions precisely as the capitalist food system has always worked; concentrating power in the hands of a privileged minority and passing off the social and environmental "externalities" disproportionately on to racially stigmatized groups."

Harper and Holt-Gímenez further established that, "Recognizing racism as foundational in today's capitalist food system helps explain why people of color suffer disproportionately from its environmental externalities, labor abuses, resource inequities and diet related diseases. It also helps explain why many of the promising alternatives such as land trusts, farmers' markets, and community-supported agriculture tend to be dominated by people who are privileged by whiteness (Guthman 2012). Making these alternatives readily accessible to people of color requires a social commitment to racial equity and a fearless commitment to social justice."

The above is merely a glimpse into this subject, as each marginalized community has its own specific struggles and means of survival in a world that riddled with injustices against them by default. Thus, understanding the intersections that an individual may face, historical and cultural influences, and how that may prevent a community from openly embracing veganism is just one way that the mainstream vegan movement can begin to form a true understanding of anti-oppression and what it means to be aware of the work that needs to be done before expecting non-white communities to readily embrace the vegan message and lifestyle. However, understanding takes us only so far. Actually putting in the work towards a just society, where veganism is actually accessible should be the ultimate goal of our movement.

In addition, it is vital that the vegan movement focus its already limited resources on vegan education as a whole and reject single-issue campaigns to ensure advocacy on behalf of all nonhuman animals and prevent the targeting and thus, the otherization of already marginalized communities of color. Author Saryta Rodríguez (2015) has noted that both humans and nonhumans are routinely otherized. They are both "criticized and punished for being different while their abundant similarities to the 'superior' group are ignored. Both have been oppressed, denied basic right to family and freedom, and forced to work (and even die) for the benefit of the 'superior' group." Within the vegan movement, otherization routinely occurs each time animal-focused activism targets a specific community for the ways in which it slaughters or exploits nonhuman animals. This is a cheap and ineffective tactic that only serves to further marginalize communities already seen as different.

All animal exploitation is wrong. All animal slaughter is wrong. When we single out specific communities, we merely close them off to the vegan message, which should be one that *all* animal exploitation is wrong – not just some. To pick and choose between groups of people to target for their cultural practices and their specific choice of animal to exploit is racist and bigoted when the human majority is culpable in the exploitation of other animals, regardless of species and methods involved. Otherization is not only a barrier that we must break down on behalf of nonhumans; it is also a commonly practiced form of human oppression that the vegan movement must openly reject. In summary, only through consistent anti-oppression will veganism be allowed to spread from the fringe movement that is currently is. Vegans must be aware, educated, and involved in the fight for human rights to elevate nonhuman rights. Consistency in anti-oppression within our movement does not mean decentering nonhumans from their own movement. It means creating an environment where marginalized communities are not further oppressed and otherized by the actions of the movement.

## Moving Towards Consistency as a Movement

The reality is that the majority of mainstream vegan/animal rights advocacy groups do not incorporate a consistent anti-oppression approach or intersectional understanding in their advocacy.

Yes, veganism is a movement FOR nonhuman animals; however, can vegans truly spread their message on their behalf if vegans themselves refuse to acknowledge that oppression is also very real for many humans? In the quest for animal rights and justice, should vegans not take care to not further oppress humans with their movement?

People of color cannot leave their skin color at the door because it dictates their very existence. Disabled people cannot simply ignore their disabilities because they affect their daily lives. People who live life under poverty cannot simply ignore their struggle for survival. People who experience discrimination because of their sexual orientation or gender cannot simply ignore part of who they are.

Now imagine being someone who experiences any or several forms of oppression because they are part of one or more than one oppressed group. Imagine encountering representatives of the animal rights movement, who tell you that your own oppression doesn't matter. Imagine being part of an oppressed group and seeing a movement that claims to be about justice protecting...your oppressors!

Would you want to be part of it?

Probably not.

Do we really want to be a group that claims to be about justice while taking part in and excusing racism, sexism, homophobia, ableism, sizeism, classism, transphobia, Islamophobia, ageism, etc. and alienating anyone who experiences those things?

Adopting a consistent anti-oppression and pro-intersectional approach does not take away from nonhuman animals. In fact, it achieves the opposite. When we oppose all oppression, and create a movement that is safe for the oppressed, we raise the voices of nonhuman animals even higher.

## Inclusiveness and Support of Vegans of Color

When supporting vegans of color and attempting to advocate a veganism that is consistently anti-oppression and understanding of others' struggles, one needs to recognize that, as a vegan that is *not* a vegan of color, your lived experiences and culture will be drastically different under a society where systematic oppression is the given. The same can be true for communities of color, themselves since our cultures are drastically different and the types of oppression we face are uniquely dependent on the race or culture. It is important to recognize when to "stay in your lane" and take a step back to let vegans of color address issues that affect their own communities.

When you think about the mainstream animal rights campaigns, one thing you may notice is the overrepresentation of campaigns that target people of color and specific cultures – dog meat, whaling, cock fighting, etc. (Vegans of color also make up a very small percentage of the vegan community in terms of visibility, yet, as previously noted, people of color make up the majority of the world's population.) This often turns into demonizing that specific race or culture when *all* cultures take part in the exploitation of other animals.

Vegans of color are aware of animal rights issues that affect their own communities, and the majority of these vegans around the world are working towards issues that affect them directly within their own communities. It is vital that one recognizes, in the attempt to raise the voices of other animals, that it is no one's role to speak over vegans of color when it comes to their own communities and experiences.

Most importantly, one needs to ASK these communities how they can best be supported. Defer conversations to vegans of color from these cultures and avoid claiming false victories by focusing on the condemnation of cultures of color while animal exploitation in white or mostly-white communities goes unchallenged.

So, what *can* you do to be consistently inclusive of anti-oppression and supportive to vegans of color?

- **When vegans of color speak, LISTEN** and amplify their voices in conversations and in the movement. Invite vegans of color to be part of conversations that affect them. This is important to keep in mind when discussing topics that involve people of color in articles, YouTube videos, etc. However, do NOT tokenize people of color. We are not all the same, nor do we have the same experiences as vegans. Involve diverse communities and individuals in your conversations of pro-intersectionality in veganism as it relates to people of color. Vegans of color are part of the vegan movement, and it is vital that the movement stop focusing on the "white" experience and defining itself by it. However, diversity is not enough; truly listening and creating change through dialogue and implementing changes is vital. Author Saryta Rodríguez further explores the concept of tokenization on page 100.

- **Recognize that your perception and experience of the world is completely different to that of a vegan of color or vegan from any other marginalized community of which you yourself**

**are not part**. Nzinga Young (2016) suggested that non-black vegans focus on food safety and accessibility in communities affected by food deserts, as an example, to help make veganism accessible. However, it is important to ASK what a specific community needs instead of assuming one knows what they need. Step outside of the vegan movement and join other anti-oppression efforts. Only then will you begin to understand how consistency in anti-oppression for all is vital in our fight for nonhuman justice.

- **Whole Foods markets, recipe books made up of obscure and often expensive ingredients, and meals focused on faux meat alternatives are not the way to help the rest of the world go vegan.** Accessibility— whether monetary, temporal, or relating to physical or mental ability— are real issues that affect many communities of color. Seek a wide variety of resources that are specific to different races and marginalized communities (by those communities for those communities).

For example, do not give white-centered veganism resources to a black person. Instead refer them to material specifically by black vegans for black vegans and for people of color by people of color. This is part of deferring conversations to the appropriate community and amplifying voices of color. If these resources do not exist, approach specific communities of color and support their advocacy through volunteer work, monetary support, or whichever way they specify your skills may be helpful to help them create their own resources.

- **Do not use people of color as targets for a campaign.** Focus on vegan education as a whole.

- **Defer culturally sensitive conversations to those actually affected by those issues or to those from those specific cultures affected by the topic at hand.** In short, stay in your lane, especially on issues that are not represented in your own culture. Recognize and commit to the understanding that you will never know more about another culture than someone from that culture. Do not speak over vegans of color.

- **Never use the historical oppression of people of color or any historically oppressed group to draw similarities within our fight for nonhuman animals.** Linking animal suffering to African slavery or the Holocaust is unacceptable unless you are from the affected community. Using historical dates that highlight abolition of slavery or any other historically oppressive moment in time to promote animal rights through the experiences of people of color is also unacceptable. Although the analogies may make sense to you in some way, comparing oppressions to invoke empathy for nonhumans is NEVER ok to do to promote veganism. Comparing oppressions of humans and nonhumans erases the past and present experience of people of color, which are very much still oppressed.

Not only is this erasure offensive, but linking human and nonhuman oppression is also seen akin to comparing humans to nonhumans when such comparisons have been traditionally used to dehumanize oppressed communities of color. Yes, we vegans see ourselves as equal to other animals in terms of their right to live freely from exploitation, but many communities of color, unsure of what veganism even means or stands for outside of a "privileged white movement," will not understand or agree.

Think back to the time before you were vegan and unaware of what your choices supported or meant and how little veganism made sense when you were unaware of what it meant or stood for. It's also important to remember that human and nonhuman oppressions are not the equivalent. Aph Ko (2017) clarifies, for example, that "we shouldn't compare black oppression to nonhuman oppression because they aren't "like" each other; they just have a common source of oppression, which is systemic white human violence."

- **Never use people of color to justify the oppression of anyone.** It IS possible to work towards anti-speciesism while being pro-intersectional and anti-oppression. Don't use your solidarity with marginalized humans to reject veganism, even if those marginalized humans cannot go fully vegan at the moment due to access, mental health or other issues. Your commitment to social justice of any kind should not be contingent on the individual or societal circumstances of others.

Conversely, in order to work towards this, we must be mindful of the "as is possible and practicable" part of the definition of veganism. In other words, don't use your commitment to justice for nonhumans as an excuse to ignore or belittle injustices faced by humans. Those that fervently support the "nonhumans first" ideal will only dig their heels in deeper against embracing a pro-intersectional and consistently anti-oppression view of veganism, where human rights are also taken into consideration. At the same time, this will also result in people of color being less open to the vegan message.

- **Learn about other cultures and the issues that affect them**. Then, get out there and work to fix those issues. Remember working against racism and all other "-isms" is part of creating a just and fair society for all. Some questions to consider in your quest to educate yourself: What forms of oppression do Asians, Latin, Black, and Indigenous communities face? How can you work to fight these oppressions in your community by supporting these communities and their efforts? What have vegans of color indicated that will help make veganism more accessible to them and their communities?

- **Openly reject vegans that support or take part in racism.** Actions speak louder than words, and empowering racists to continue their work in our movement— especially when they refuse to learn and evolve from such hurtful stances simply because they are well-known activists or heads of organizations— only serves to show vegans of color that we do not matter in the vegan movement despite being vital in the creation of a vegan world since the majority of people on Earth are people of color. The same goes to anyone that partakes in any form of human oppression, whether homophobia, xenophobia, ableism, Islamophobia, classism, etc. When you continue to accept the presence of human oppressors, give them a platform and/or openly interact with them, you show oppressed people what side you are really on.

Seriously, do the work. Otherwise, we, both humans and nonhumans, all lose.

## Intersectionality versus Diversity: A Note to Vegan Organizations

So far, we have discussed what it means to be anti-speciesist in a nonhuman-centered movement, as well as how to be pro-intersectional and the importance of acknowledging that veganism will differ for marginalized communities and individuals. How a group or organization embraces these concepts as a whole will also determine its success in helping other communities embrace veganism.

A seasoned activist and published author, Saryta Rodríguez has spent a large part of their advocacy examining how to bridge the gap between human and nonhuman animal rights. Through their social justice advocacy, Rodríguez writes:

*Discussions of intersectionality typically focus on the* **actualities that** *oppressions share a common structure, and in order to fight oppression of any kind we must be cognizant of this overarching structure." Furthermore, the plight of members of more than one marginalized group cannot be fully understood and therefore addressed without considering the interplay between oppressions that apply to them. For instance, the plight of black women cannot be understood fully by feminist theory or race theory alone, but requires examination of the intersection between race-based and gender-based discrimination.*

*There are two fundamental items missing from mainstream intersectional dialogue, which are worrisome. The first and simplest of these to state outright is **that it isn't enough to understand intersectional theory to call oneself or one's organization intersectional; you must regularly employ an intersectional praxis in your activism.** With respect to the Vegan Ethos, for instance, it is important not only to understand intellectually that humans are animals and that animal liberation is human liberation, but also to contribute to that by abstaining from products that are the result of human slave labor, kidnapping or other cruel practices that harm humans— and engaging in protests and other disruptive forms of campaigning to bring attention to these abuses. A strawberry may be meat- and dairy-free, but depending on where it came from it may not actually be vegan in the fullest sense of the word (causing the least amount of harm; created in a manner that is just).*

*Ethical consistency matters. You can't expect someone to take your advice about not eating, wearing or otherwise exploiting nonhumans seriously when you engage in behaviors that blatantly contribute to the exploitation of humans.*

*The second item I want to address here is that **intersectionality and diversity are not synonyms.** A group can be diverse without being intersectional, and vice-versa. Within the spectrum of diversity, it is worth noting that a group can also be racially diverse without being* *gender-diverse, gender-diverse while lacking diversity in age, and so forth.*

*To simplify matters, let's focus on racial diversity for a moment. The following chart outlines four possibilities with respect to vegan advocacy groups' commitment to both racial diversity and intersectionality:*

| | Racially Diverse | Lacking Racial Diversity |
|---|---|---|
| **Intersectional** | A vegan advocacy group with many POC members as well as white members, equally focusing on human and nonhuman issues. Such a group actively pursues ways to improve the lot of various oppressed humans. *Examples:* Food Empowerment Project; the alliance between the Black Lives Matter movement and the Boycott, Divestment, Sanctions movement. | A vegan advocacy group that is largely racially homogenous, equally focusing on human and nonhuman issues. Although intersectional groups tend to be racially diverse, this need not be so. In my opinion, racial diversity is essential for the development of a truly intersectional organization— where the voices of members of each race are equally heard and POCs are not tokenized. |

| | A vegan advocacy group with many POC members as well as white members, focusing almost exclusively on nonhuman issues by employing rhetoric and strategies that exclude many human groups. In such groups, POC members are commonly tokenized. *Examples*: granting public titles to POC members without allowing them to freely fulfill their roles; using one POC's approval of a strategy against complaints by other POCs that the strategy is offensive. | A vegan advocacy group that is largely racially homogenous (whether that means mostly-white, mostly-black, mostly-Hispanic, etc.), focusing almost exclusively on nonhuman issues and employing rhetoric and strategies that exclude large swaths of the human population. Regrettably, this is the most common type of group found in the mainstream Animal Liberation Movement, and the homogeneity is typically of a mostly-white nature. |
|---|---|---|
| **Not Intersectional** | | |

*If we continue to conflate diversity with intersectionality, the end result is that we will create all of these strong, talented, inspiring, and diverse communities with which to campaign for one piece of the puzzle...while continuing to fail to address the other pieces. Making sure the brown-to-white ratio is reasonable (or the LGBTQP+-to-straight ratio, trans-to-cis ratio, etc.) is not what intersectionality is all about, and that goal, while itself not always easy to obtain, is nevertheless much easier to reach than achieving true intersectionality as an organization.*

*In their essay entitled "Black Lives, Black Life," Aph and Syl Ko (2017) speak on the issue of valuing black bodies over black ideas, and thus not truly valuing black lives. What I'm getting at here is similar, though not specific to the black community– that by conflating intersectionality and diversity, mainstream vegan advocacy groups prioritize the inclusion of black and brown bodies into a particular setting (or trans and queer bodies, or bodies with varying abilities) without going the extra mile to include their ideas.*

*Letting people from marginalize communities speak is wonderful, but how often, after they speak, do you actually take the advice they give you? Change the way you're currently doing something? Read whatever source they recommended? Challenge yourself not just to provide an ear for folks to talk into, but to slacken your attachment to your own beliefs and preferred strategies (which are, to an extent, informed by socially unjust institutions in which Reason really means what-white-cis-men-said-a-hundred-years-ago) and allow yourself to actually be influenced by the ideas of marginalized folk. Not just spoken ideas, either– which is why I mentioned the recommended reading. Many established figures in the social sciences frequently quote or refer to the findings of white cis men. True intersectionality cannot be achieved when only one group of people is telling us how to achieve it. We need thinkers from these communities to guide us in the conclusions we draw.*

*As an individual, intersectionality is easy enough, though it can be time consuming. As an organization, it is much more complicated than simply reaching out to different types of people; you have to make time in your schedule to support other organizations and/or commit to diversifying the focal points of each of your own events (i.e. hosting one demonstration every other month that is about a cause other that your usual). No social justice movement can truly succeed until it acknowledges that it is just one piece of a larger Movement for a Just Society. For a deeper understanding of why this is the case, John Sanbonmatsu's "The Postmodern Prince: Critical Theory, Left Strategy, and the Making of a New Political Subject" is a resource to look into. Organizations that insist on intensive internal programming, requiring members to appear at their events multiple times per week, disable activists from engaging in other causes and thereby truly expanding the Vegan Ethos to encompass human animals who may not (yet) be vegan.*

*Diversity is fundamental to effective intersectionality. It is by focusing on diversity that we ensure that our strategies are maximally effective and minimally offensive. A common failure among campaigns against the use of dog leather in China, for example, is a lack of Chinese voices. The same is true of campaigns attacking the use of animals for religious sacrifice, dolphin and whaling abuses in Japan, and other animal abuses that are considered "un-American." Without diversity, the lines become blurred and those outside of the animal liberation community—or even within it— may perceive not a group of humans standing up for nonhumans but rather one group of humans asserting its ethical superiority over another group of humans.*

*A diversity of voices in legislative decision-making is fundamental to ensuring that inherently racist and hypocritical legislation is not passed under the guise of protecting nonhumans. For instance, in Arizona in 2009 a bill was passed banning horse tripping and other key features of the charreada, or Mexican rodeo. While these practices are indeed cruel, to call this strictly an animal liberation victory is misleading; it is also a triumph of racism. The bill explicitly excuses/protects acts that are considered a "standard" part of the (American) rodeo, in which animals are allegedly "unharmed." Were this truly a measure to protect animals, American rodeos would have been banned right alongside charreadas. Instead, this legislation is at once hypocritical, in that it allows Americans to continue being cruel to animals for the sake of entertainment, and a heinous effort to promote negative racial stereotypes. It reinforces the Us vs. Them dynamic without actually addressing the fundamental question of why nonhumans are being treated violently by any race of human for the sake of "entertainment."*

*The best hope we have of preventing these and similar measures from passing is to push ever forward towards complete animal liberation and call out racist initiatives masked as liberationist initiatives whenever and wherever we encounter them. We mustn't be too quick to celebrate any motion that appears to protect animals, but instead always consider the Big Picture and ask ourselves whether the precedent being set is All animals deserve to be free or*

*We will free some animals while oppressing others—*
*including humans— and hope you do not notice."*

## Mindfully Raising Their Voices

Nonhuman animals are not voiceless. This statement should not be controversial, yet it is. Claiming they are voiceless ignores that they are individuals that exist in their own right, within their own communities or natural environments, with their own languages and lives independent of the human experience. Vegans should be centered on working against oppression. In order to be the most conscientious and efficient allies we can be, we need to recognize that our role is to **raise the voices and presence of ALL nonhuman animals** in a world in which they are silenced and ignored behind closed doors. This isn't about us, and this isn't just about the species for which it is easiest to advocate. Vegan advocacy is about justice, and our goal should be clearly focused not on reducing nonhuman oppression, but on eradicating it— which involves acknowledging the voice, will, desires and rights of all individuals, even when we cannot understand the language they speak.

In closing, veganism as a clearly defined term matters. What we expend our energy advocating for, how we treat oppression itself and how we address other oppressed groups matter as well. How we choose to invoke these individual facets of our advocacy has massive

31

implications, which either hurt or aid our movement achieve its goal. The direction in which we move from here on will be the deciding factor in whether or not we achieve justice for all animals.

## Cited Works

Bowleg, L (2008) When Black+ lesbian+ woman≠ Black lesbian woman: The methodological challenges of qualitative and quantitative intersectionality research. *Sex roles*: 59(5-6), 312-325

Crenshaw, K (2015) *Why Intersectionality Can't Wait*, Washington Post: https://www.washingtonpost.com/news/in-theory/wp/2015/09/24/why-intersectionality-cant-wait

Harper, A B (2016) *Food Deserts 101*: http://www.sistahvegan.com/food-deserts

Harper, A B & Holt-Gímenez, E (2016) *Food-Systems-Racism: From Mistreatment to Transformation:* https://foodfirst.org/wp-content/uploads/2016/03/DR1Final.pdf

Gorman, S (2016) Voices from the boundary line: The Australian Football League's Indigenous team of the century. In *Indigenous People, Race Relations and Australian Sport*: 100-111

Guthman, J (2012) *If They Only Knew: Color Blindness and Universalism in California Alternative Food Institutions.* In Taking Food Public: Redefining Foodways in a Changing World (New York, London: Routledge): 211–23

Ko, A & S (2017*) Aphro-ism, Essays on Pop Culture, Feminism, and Black Veganism from Two sisters*: https://aphro-ism.com

Marks, K (2013) *Australia Takes Symbolic Step to Recognizing Aboriginal Rights*, Independent: http://www.independent.co.uk/news/world/australasia/australia-takes-symbolic-step-to-recognising-aboriginal-rights-8493844.html

Robinson, M (2017) Personal communication.

Rodríguez, S (2015) *Until Every Animal Is Free*: 59-60

Wrenn, C L and, R (2013) A Critique of Single-Issue Campaigning and the Importance of Comprehensive Abolitionist Vegan Advocacy, *Food, Culture & Society* 16 (4): 651-668

Young, N (2016) *Here's Why Black People Don't Go Vegan*, Huffington Post: http://www.huffingtonpost.com/nzinga-young/heres-why-black-people-do_b_10028678.html

## 2 VEGANISM THROUGH COLOR

The following pages feature the voices of vegans of color from all walks of life. You may feel understanding and empathy as you read. You may also find yourself feeling defensive, angered, and even consumed with guilt and sadness. These are all normal reactions to the discomfort of realizing how a movement we believe in has fallen short, or even how we as individuals haven't always been as effective or inclusive as we should have been. Use these complex emotions to examine your place in the movement, and the world. Challenge yourself to use whatever privilege you may have to empower nonhumans and humans alike, as well as to commit to ethical consistency in spite of whatever privileges you may lack. This is more than just a call to check your privilege; it is a call to expand your horizons. We simply ask that you arm yourself with the tools, resources and resolve necessary to help the mainstream vegan movement reach farther than ever before.

# Poetry

## *White Poem*

### By Meneka Repka

In the summer, the mist hangs hot and oppressive
The walls are white, the sheets are white
And Egyptian cotton

On this day, the pure white bone china teacup
Is full and steaming
With condensation crying down its sides

Next to the tea are the following:
Sugar cubes like diamonds in the hazy light
Dark chocolate, and silver spoons

Somewhere in the distance, a wind chime tinkles
There is no evidence of harm here
Everything is quiet and peaceful and white

These things are the height of civility
There is no flesh
And the white things are absolved of cruelty

Outside the house of white
The bodies toil together; they hear the hissing whistles
And smell the dank air

Here, the cloying whiteness
Is crusted thickly with blood and decay
And the ivory keys are slightly out of tune

*****

In this poem, I examine the pervasiveness of whiteness in mainstream and dominant vegan movements. I am especially interested in the ways in which vegan consumer choices are marketed through a linguistic distancing from cruelty (i.e. "cruelty free"). As many vegans of color have pointed out, foods that are vegan are not necessarily "cruelty free," as these products are often a part of a capitalist system and oppress someone (frequently people of color) in the line of production.

I reference foods that are commonly consumed by vegans, but are rarely considered through a racialized lens: tea, sugar, and chocolate. I challenge the idea of veganism as a more "evolved" state of being, which assumes that the eschewal of nonhuman animal biproducts is the highest level of morality.

Finally, I wanted this work to be reminiscent of the intersections of race with slaughterhouse work. The contrast of supervisory roles in slaughterhouses with the work of killing is conveyed similarly through the pristine nature of offices compared to the dangerous and repulsive kill floor.

## *Through OUR Eyes, In OUR Words*

### By Destiny Whitaker

We know what it is before we can read. We witnessed it before we were of the age to speak. We could not pronounce the word if we knew of it, nor could we fathom why it existed and sabotaged us because of it.

But alas, it does.

Privilege.

Something they don't want to acknowledge. They try to equate their struggle to ours. Invalidate us and publicly debate if and when our lives matter.

They proclaim their disdain, but privately shake hands with whom they said they'd never speak to again.

Given resources and funds that we'll never see. Travel the world and seven seas. Simplifying things that seem as minuscule as grocery budgeting and financial distributing.

We are the beings who are often silenced and desired to be rendered voiceless. Our educating seen as misbehaving.

The spaces in which we know our voices are needed we will always stay within. Loud and proud we shall be.

We relate and remember the past, present, and not only hope, but fight for a peaceful future.

Despite our trials and tribulations. The exclusion, judgment, and *no*'s we receive - We remember our fellow like-minded beings - Melanin and all, and we keep on keeping on.

In order to reach our Destiny; Our Safe Haven. Our Sanctuary. Our Sacred Sanctuary.

Must non-POCs choose to ignore our culture, religion, financial situation, lack of privileges (regarding activism and opportunities), physical and mental health, etc. and yet profit from making vegan versions of our cultural dishes and appropriating our culture itself?

Some say that veganism is not meant to be intersectional because humans have a voice and other animals do not. Yes, we do have a voice; yet others seldom listen to our words, cries, and pleas. Therefore, we are rendered silent more often than not.

There were *human zoos* that showcased Africans. The 4th Of July offers nothing to celebrate for Black and Indigenous people. The list goes on and on, and it is not only the past that displays our lack of rights; the present does as well.

I hope this poem will inspire other People of Color

(specifically Black People) to use their voice and help non-POCs realize that their movement can neither succeed nor truly be just without the inclusion of these voices.

Educate. Educate. Educate. Educate yourself and others. Hold people accountable. Let those who try to erase the voices of people of color know that their actions will not be embraced nor tolerated in our movement.

Together, we will progress within our movement if we truly work against all oppression.

Veganism must be intersectional, or else it is doomed to failure.

# Short Reflections

## *A Veganism for Us*

### By Michelle Carrera

The sandwiches were packed, the oranges in their sack, the water bottles cooled; we were ready to meet people! Our old van drove through the main street in Dover, New Hampshire, and we spotted a pair of folks. We were able to park a few feet from them.

"Are you ready, Ollie?" I asked my six-year-old.

"Yeah, let's do it!" he said.

"Hey, folks, would you like a sandwich?"

"Oh my God, girl, *yes!*"

"They're vegan and quite delicious!"

"Ok" the man shrugged and took the meal. Within a few seconds, we had a crowd of about eighteen people asking us what we were giving. One young man approached us and, when we said we had sandwiches, he said "No thank you. I don't eat meat." Of course, I instantly lit up and almost yelled, "It's vegan! We're vegan!"

The light transferred to him. "No way! A vegan sandwich?!" Soon, we had given out all of our supplies, and stayed talking to our new vegan friend. He proceeded to tell us that it's tough out there, especially for a vegan.

None of the shelters or soup kitchens offers vegan alternatives, so it's hard to find something to eat— and it's even harder to go to the crowds that advocate for veganism because he doesn't feel like he is accepted there.

His exact words were, "I fight for the animals, but nobody fights for me."

It's a story that is familiar to us. Throughout the course of Chilis on Wheels's lifespan, we've encountered many vegans of color experiencing hardship, who tell similar stories. No options in the shelters and lack of support from the communities they belonged to… and that's on top of being singled out for caring about the animals and being vegan. Neither here nor there. Neither with the vegans, because of being a homeless person of color, nor with the homeless people of color, because of being vegan.

That's a lonely place to be.

It's a problem we have in the vegan movement, when people feel like they can't count on the support from other vegans and even face outright rejection from the community. How can people be asked to join a movement that does not want them?

As someone who grew up with privilege but lost it— someone who grew up colonized in Puerto Rico, attending an all-English school on an island that speaks Spanish, and asked to watch cable shows so I could imitate how Americans talk and lose my accent— I understand the feeling of being "neither here nor there."

Straddling two worlds, sometimes three or four, as our lives and identities are not binary, and our communities don't seem to overlap. I went vegan in Puerto Rico at a time where there was no vegan culture there. I didn't know one other single vegan, and when I moved to New York City in 2004, I met many vegans, but none of color. I never experienced outright hostility, but I did experience dismissal. The increasing importance placed in the consumeristic aspect of veganism shut me out of the conversation, as I did not share the means to participate in that aspect of vegan culture. Get a group of vegans together, and they talk about the latest restaurants that are vegan, the latest products on the market— in short, the latest way that they, as vegans, spent money.

I'm converging lack of financial privilege to ethnicity, as they are related. The 2015 poverty rate for Black folks was at 24.1 percent; for Hispanic people, 21.4 percent; and for White people, 9.1 percent. Because of systemic racism, redlining, and unfair wage gaps, among other things, people of color live in poverty in increasing numbers over their white counterparts. Thus, the consumer culture of veganism hurts people of color who wish to fight for the animals, but who feel shut out when conversations and outings revolve around pricey restaurants, conferences, and products. Of course, when other participants actively reject their contribution to the movement by making outright racist and classist statements, people also walk away.

How can we change? How can we convince white

vegans to allow us in their movement?

We don't. Because it isn't solely their movement. Because veganism doesn't belong to any one race of people.

We build upon the movement ourselves. We do not ask permission. We build our own networks of support, our own culture of inclusiveness, our own safe spaces. Chilis on Wheels has been doing this in NYC, and now we've taken it in the road with TheVTeamTour, where we met Julio, the vegan homeless man in Dover. We are building communities in which we can come together, share a vegan meal, and build lasting relationships of support to one another. We build each other up with whatever privileges we may have, so that we don't have to choose between fighting for animals and fighting for each other. I am encouraged to see other communities also building their own spaces in cities across the country, and I take inspiration from their successes.

I gave Julio a hug before I left on the van, and promised him that we'd keep fighting so that we can keep building the world we know is possible, kind and just for everyone.

## *Class, Color, & Compassion*

## By Melissa John-Charles Carrillo

My friends and family of color are working-class, compassionate people. I grew up in a household in which money was always an issue. My mother raised my sisters and I to be strong Afro-Latinx women and to look out for others less fortunate than us.

Being a low-income family in the UK, we children were entitled to free school meals. I would eat whatever was on offer – lamb cobbler, chips and gravy, chicken pie. At sixteen, I started to think that my love for other animals meant that I could in no way justify eating them. So I stopped. The veganism came two years later, after I read more and reflected further about the movement and the suffering human animals cause others.

It was hard for my mother to understand, but, almost twenty years later, I think she recognizes that my veganism stems from her moral lessons on empathy for others. My Venezuelan mother— with her wonderful cooking of lentils, kidney beans, plantain, rice with grated carrots, *arepas* handmade from maize flour, and beautiful salads— taught me that so much of the food I grew up with is cruelty-free already. Nevertheless, the traditional Latinx foods like *quesillo* (crème caramel) and all of the meat and fish are seen as healthy, a way of life, a comfort, culturally important, and affordable; no alternative to that is really recognized.

My family still struggles financially. Until a person has lived this way, it is difficult to understand how basic necessities like food are depoliticized; that it is too much to consider that what is on your plate was once a life or that the milk in your mug of tea was taken from mothers who only wanted to bring up their babies to be strong.

I think that it is easy for vegans – especially ones who aren't of color – to assume that people of color, namely working-class people of color, aren't worth talking to about veganism. This is indolent and patronizing. I don't have all of the answers myself, but I think a start would be to assure all people that their basic nutrients can still be met in a vegan diet; that comforting food after a 12-hour shift at work can be vegan; that vegan food can be affordable, and that we have many foods at our disposal that are already vegan; and that people of color come from a long succession of survivors of pain and struggle, and compassion for others is key to our identity.

However, this would first mean that vegans that are not of colour must recognize and understand that people of colour come from very different backgrounds, opportunities, and cultures, which affect how they view food and how they make daily choices unrelatedly to compassion.

## Parallel Oppressions

**By Rayven Whitaker**

Our world is not in tip-top shape, to say the least. As of late, my mind has been drawn towards two specific issues within it and how the two mirror each other. I stand for black lives, and I am very proud to do so. I stand for human rights in general and animal rights, as well.

There is a connection between veganism and the black community when I view the two separately. I am an ethical vegan. I went vegan purely to help put a stop to the cruelty brought upon animals.

When learning about the Black Lives Matter movement specifically, I became aware of what surrounded me. Violence due to irrational thinking. Violence carried out by uniforms, egos, and skin color. Police brutality was evident, and there was no way around invalidating the injustice.

Veganism further broadened my nascent perspective. The world became much more than a simple globe to me. It was an oppressive reality. One where oppression went beyond one minority. The suffering was mutual between the relations shared by those who fought for the right to breathe without being assumed dangerous and the beings who fought to be more than meal scraps at the breakfast table.

There is a brilliant documentary within the depths of the Internet and elsewhere entitled "Earthlings." To me,

the opening scene was and is utterly terrifying—
something sickening, yet beautiful once the feeling of
rising bile begins to subside.

> "It is the human earthling who tends
> to dominate the earth, oftentimes
> treating other fellow earthlings and
> living beings as mere objects. This is
> what is meant by 'speciesism.' By
> analogy with racism and sexism,
> speciesism is a prejudice or attitude or
> bias in favor of the interests of the
> members of one's own species and
> against those of members of other
> species."

> -Narrator of "Earthlings", Joaquin
> Phoenix

These words played in my mind just as your favorite
record would; only this record sat on a side table whilst
having nails drawn upon it. The imagery only added to
the tragedy of this beautiful record. The world was no
longer as fair as it had seemed weeks ago. It was no
longer as easy to stumble upon this "world peace" for
which we all seem to yearn.

With this newfound information, what was I to do? I
could ignore it, yes; but what would that solve? Who was
I to preach a need for peace when ignoring a light shining
towards it?

At this point in my life, there is nothing prohibiting me from rejecting animal cruelty when it comes to what I consume. I have the privilege of having the resources to grasp not only the concept of peace for one group but also that of peace for multiple groups at once. At the end of the documentary, I was left in a room with minimal sunlight, a glowing laptop screen, and my own thoughts.

The mocking sounds from slaughterhouse workers as they forced a calf to leave the comfort of his mother's warmth replayed over and over in my mind. As someone still in school, my thoughts kept going back to the realization that bullying was a challenge that went beyond shouts of slurs exchanged by school kids; it is still a shocking awareness for me to grasp. The visuals placed before me showed that people behave towards other animals as oppressively as they do towards each other. Seeing speciesism and racism along with other forms of human oppression aligned was very eye opening. While there are differences, the similarities were much too loud for me to ignore.

As a human being with many labels following me, I am— slowly, but surely— finding my voice. I have become more outspoken against the injustices that are forced upon both humans and other animals. I've chosen to embrace veganism as an act against the injustice of other animals and to work in my local community on environmental issues, such as air pollution with the organization Mom's Clean Air Force. I have also committed myself to advocacy on behalf of Save DACA (Deferred Action for Childhood Arrivals), No Dakota Access Pipeline, and the Freedom of the Press.

It can be a bit challenging when attempting to find the balance in activism, and although it is overwhelming at times, I am thankful for the awareness I have found. Through this consciousness, I am hoping for the most lovely and substantial of journeys as I put in my part towards creating a just world for all the oppressed.

## *Reflections: A Journey Towards Veganism in a Muslim Upbringing*

## By Shazia Juna

The green slopes of Northern Wales looked like gentle dragons snoozing in the light rain. I felt myself absorbed in the music of the train weaving through the landscape, a bit hesitant about the forthcoming family dinner. I was very much looking forward to seeing my father after so many weeks, a much anticipated visit home from university. I had kept my transition from vegetarianism to veganism fairly low key. I thought at least it would not be as difficult as when I tried to become a vegetarian at age seventeen.

My mind wandered back to my final Islamic Studies class, which I had taken while living in Karachi, Pakistan. Mrs. Nayab was a rather stern teacher, and invited the "right" questions from the students. That day, she wrote a few Quranic verses relating to the mercy of Allah and introducing the concept of Halal foods. After her sermon, she invited us to ask questions. She seemed to be in a fairly good mood, so I bravely raised my hand. She gestured to go ahead, so I stood up and declared that surely we can exclude some foods from the list of permitted foods on moral grounds, such as animal products.

She rushed in my direction, and I could see only anger in her eyes. She slapped me across my face twice, with words that pierced my heart like arrows: 'You will regress from Islam', she spat furiously, 'Who do you think you are, to declare the standard of morality?'

I stood there, numb and shocked in disbelief. Later, I walked home quietly, unsure about the concept of a merciful Allah allowing the killing of animals. Of course, I knew that, with every breath I took, I killed so many organisms. Life thrives on death.

After that lesson, most of my colleagues ignored me. I never told my family about this incident, or the ones that had preceded it. Of course, I felt sadness and fear that I would get hit again. But mostly, I just felt numb and ultimately, isolated. However, despite everything, I was still determined.

By the time I got home, I had decided to ask my parents— again— if they were ok with my being a vegetarian. My mother was "fine" with it, but said that if the prophet Muhammad ate meat, who are we to say it is unkind to do so? My father was more liberal, but informed me that I could not make any major life decisions until I was eighteen years old. My dad was always worried about my health, and wanted me to eat enough protein. I never wanted to hurt my parents' feelings, and they had enough trouble dealing with a daughter who was more fascinated by sciences and space travel than jewellery and clothes. I never got along so well with my older sisters, and I was a bit of a loner.

A year later, we moved back to England. I was now age nineteen, and I reminded my father about his promise. Reluctantly, he agreed to accept my vegetarianism, and I felt that I had been set free.

Twenty-four years later, I prepared to tell my elderly father that I was a vegan.

As I walked home, I took deep breaths and organized all the nutritional information in my head. I also checked for the vegan banana cake that I had made for him and was carrying in my bag. The moment finally arrived; I told my father that I was vegan, and I was ready to show him some publications. As I opened my bag, my father held my hand. 'I'm proud of you' he said, softly. As I shared the cake with my father and siblings, I thought to myself that there is mercy and kindness after all.

*****

*"Reflections: A Journey towards Veganism in a Muslim Upbringing"* is a synthesis of my experience of transitioning into vegetarianism and, later, veganism as a female person of color raised in a Muslim family. My intention for writing this piece is to highlight how anxious and excluded I felt because of conflicting personal ethical choices and sociocultural norms. Through my journey towards veganism, I was met with unconditional love and joy from my parents, yet faced prejudice and exclusion from my teachers and colleagues.

## *Vegan Misappropriations of Hinduism*

### By Rama Ganesan

Although I was raised as a Hindu, as a non-believer, I have no inherent stake in religions. I did not need religion to go vegan— or to *stay* vegan. That hasn't precluded me from experiencing forms of religion-based nonviolence advocacy as an exertion of power and commonly accepted disrespect. At least, this is how it feels when someone from "the outside" tells me how to employ and view my own religion and cultural practices. These perhaps well-meaning advocates have a sense of entitlement, redefining and using aspects of my traditions to make their case with a level of comfort they would never accept from someone doing the same with *their* own culture.

When non-Indian vegans disclose that they are Hindu and offer their perspectives— including the assertion that yoga is *so* connected to veganism— I can predict the trajectory these conversations will take once I attempt to amend their Western views.

Some examples:

A conversation with "Iris" at an animal rights conference:

**Iris:** Oh, the way cows are treated in India is so

awful! Their stomachs are full of plastic. I must speak with someone and get them to do something about it. Hindus are supposed to worship cows, not mistreat them!

**Me:** Why do you want to tell Hindus how to practice their own religion?

**Iris:** Hinduism is my chosen religion, too. I have been a Hindu for years.

**Me:** But if there are things you do not like about Hinduism, why did you choose it to be your religion?

**Iris:** But I DO like it!

**Me:** So, if you are a Hindu, what is your caste?

**Iris:** Oh no, I don't believe in all that caste stuff.

**Me:** So, if you don't like some things about Hinduism, then why did you choose it to be your religion?

**Iris:** Oh, well, I don't know.

A conversation with "Megan" on the way back from a Vegfest:

**Megan:** I'm a Hindu, actually. Yoga and Hinduism have so much to do with veganism!

**Me:** Have you seen how Krishna is a god who drinks cow's milk? And how the Hindus believe cows give milk because they are our mothers?

**Megan:** Oh yes, I don't like that! In fact, I have written to them a couple of times, to tell them that it is not right to drink milk and they shouldn't be taking milk from cows.

**Me:** Have you written to Christians to tell them they're not treating animals right?

**Megan:** Well, no....

**Me:** Well, if you are interested in changing Hinduism, then why not change Christianity, too?

**Megan:** Oh, it's not that I'm Hindu or Christian; I'm more "spiritual"...

A conversation among white women about yoga at my fitness studio. They glance at me, the only person of color, every so often. One of the women has adopted a Sanskrit word as her name, "Ahimsa."

**Ahimsa:** Oh, yoga is just so profound.

**Teacher:** Yes, I recently studied chakras. The heart chakra is for love and the throat chakra is for communication. My friend who was having a hard time communicating with others came down with a throat infection the next day. There is just so much to all this ancient wisdom.

**Me:** You know chakras are based on pseudoscience and nonsense, right?

**Teacher:** Well, I like it!

**Me:** It's ok to like it, of course!

Ahimsa starts to say something, but then turns away. She is visibly annoyed by my comments. However, she decides not to pursue the argument.


A vegan, "Aleks," invites me to a Hare Krishna event on Facebook. I write on the event page that Hare Krishnas are never going to give up "humane" (ahimsa) milk:

**Aleks:** I want you to come to this event so *you* can tell them that taking cow's milk isn't vegan!

You get it exactly as they should.

**Me:** Why do you want to follow a religion you disagree with?

**Aleks:** Oh, well, the Bhagavad Gita speaks to me.

**Me:** You mean the treatise where a god incites humans to go into war with their siblings with the promise that their "true immortal spirit" can never die?

**Aleks:** Peace to you.

When involved in these types of exchanges with non-Indians about my own culture and religion, I purposely point out the drawbacks of Hinduism in hopes that they will realize that their perspective on Hinduism and yoga are based on Western ideologies appropriating only *aspects* of an elaborate religion and set cultural practices. In other words, their knowledge of Hinduism is based on cherry-picked sound bites aimed at confirming Western stereotypes, while anything that contradicts or challenges those stereotypes has been omitted from their Westernized Hindu "education."

I openly draw attention to the fact that Hindus think cows are mothers who *give* milk (rather than that humans *take* it), and that there has always been a caste system associated with Hinduism (contrary to Western vegan notions of equality among all life forms). I often express that elaborations around yoga are just conflated mumbo-jumbo. I also note that our holy scriptures, far from treatises on peace and love, are in fact about waging wars with one's own brothers and the abduction of women. When they insist on how spiritual and non-violent Hinduism is, I might even disclose that India is the rape capital of the world. I sometimes also add that the beef ban in India is a form of oppression by a nationalistic government and that vegetarianism is a form of upper-class purity— which is, in fact, a direct contradiction to intersectional vegan advocacy.

Often, those people who were not born Hindu but who have a desire to be Hindu feel this way based on Western misrepresentations of fetishized religious imagery. As a vegan Indian woman, I am often placed in the position where I need to remind those who attempt to explain my own religion and cultural practices to me that some of us didn't get to *choose* Hinduism. We did not get to dissect and internalize the parts that we liked while eschewing or ignoring the parts we did not. We were born into it, live it, and have inherited **all** of it.

Choosing one's own form and definition of Hindu is a clear case of cultural appropriation. Hinduism isn't a means to find some type of generic universal truth, nor is it a simple dogma to mold into the parts that fit with veganism. Hinduism, like any other religion, is an established belief system, with established traditions with which those beliefs are upheld. It is not a flexible philosophical guideline to be adapted according to individual preferences.

Imagine if we applied these same appropriations to other religions— specifically Western ones. What would that look like? Mennonites, for example, are considered part of a pacifist, non-violent faith. Sounds like veganism, since vegans believe in nonviolence towards all animals, no? Perhaps vegans should embrace and join Mennonite churches. However, Mennonites consume meat, dairy, and eggs— which contradicts adherence to nonviolence. Would it be appropriate for someone new to the religion to contact the representatives and demand they amend their religion, despite it being about more than just nonviolence, to suit the vegan narrative?

Having many of the above experiences and conversations in mind, I was both excited and anxious when I recently attended an AR conference session titled *Engaging through Religions*. I wondered if the speakers would discuss how to convincingly argue why people of certain religions should be vegan. If so, I feared that Hindus might suffer the most in misrepresentation and misunderstanding. I suspected that the Hindu woman sitting next to me, perhaps new to veganism, would feel the same sense of frustration that I did each time Hinduism was explained through a non-Hindu perspective. Surprisingly, I learned about the plant-based roots of Western religions, such as Judaism. I was intrigued to learn that so many rabbis are vegetarians who 'lean vegan.' I realized that perhaps my message in conversations about religion should be one that reinforces the fact that embracing a spiritual veganism does not automatically mean assuming an Eastern religion, such as Hinduism (or Jainism and Buddhism).

Because of this, I have become inspired to encourage others to research and study the nonviolent roots of their own religions and how they align with veganism. The more we understand these connections in other religions and cultures, the less pressure or compulsion there may be to appropriate and misrepresent Eastern religions, like my own.

# Essays

## *Intersectionality in Mi'kmaw and Settler Vegan Values*

## By Margaret Robinson

I am an Indigenous woman— a Mi'kmaw woman[1]. My people have lived in Mi'kma'ki, our territory on the east coast of what is now Canada, for over thirteen thousand years. My veganism has been shaped by my relationships with both the land and the people who share it with me. By "people," I mean not only human people, but also other animals—those Mi'kmaw elder Wanda Whitebird sometimes calls "the people who walk, the people who crawl, the people who swim, and the people who fly." In Mi'kmaq, the language of Lnu'k (the people), we refer to these folks using the phrase "all my relations." The notion that we are related to all other animals exists in the philosophical and spiritual worldview of many Indigenous nations, but I shall reflect only on what it means in my culture and to me as an individual.

A brief word about my terminology: it is possible to eat a vegan diet and not also be an animal rights activist, or to be an animal rights activist and not also be vegan. However, I see my veganism and activism as two manifestations of a similar position. For the sake of argument, I'm treating them as intrinsically related, for reasons I think will become clear. When I refer to Settler

---

[1] Mi'kmaw is the singular and adjectival form of Mi'kmaq.

veganism, I am assuming that includes a commitment to the liberation of other animals from oppression.

## Living Mi'kmaw Values

Mi'kmaw values are embedded in our oral tradition—the stories that we tell about ourselves, our history, and the lives of the animals and other beings around us. Some of my favorite stories involve Glooskap, the Mi'kmaw cultural hero. He's like our Superman. He's smart, honest, generous, respectful, and strong. Sometimes, he is portrayed as having supernatural powers; at other times, he's just a really impressive human. Our creation story tells us he was formed from the red clay of the soil and initially lacked mobility, trapped on his back in the dirt (Native American Legends: Nukumi and Fire, n.d.). This imagery reaffirms how dependent we are on the land.

The Creator frees Glooskap and creates an old woman from a dew-covered rock. This is Glooskap's grandmother, and she agrees to provide wisdom for him if he will provide food for her. She explains that she cannot live on plants and berries alone, and needs meat to survive. Glooskap calls to his friend, Marten— an animal similar to a weasel or a ferret— and asks Marten to give his life so that Glooskap's grandmother may live. Marten agrees. For this sacrifice, Glooskap makes Marten his brother. In later stories we see that Glookap and Marten (who is sometimes an animal, sometimes a little boy, and sometimes a young man) live together and Glooskap refers to Marten as "my younger brother" (Leland, 1884).

In the creation story Glooskap's grandmother snaps Marten's neck, killing him, which makes Glooskap very sad. Moved by Glooskap's mourning, the grandmother prays to the Creator, and Marten returns to life. In his place is the body of another marten, which they eat. This story encapsulates the relationship of the Mi'kmaw people with the creatures around us. Nonhuman animals are imagined as willing to provide food in return for being treated with the respect given to a brother or a friend.

One of the things I like about this version of our creation story is that, before his grandmother came along, it doesn't seem as if Glooskap ate other animals. As well, the justification for eating Martin is need, not pleasure. Glooskap's grandmother didn't want to eat Marten just because he looked tasty. So if we don't need to eat other animals to survive, there isn't a justification, within the worldview of this story, for killing them. In addition, Glooskap's sadness over Marten's death is important, since he models the appropriate response to all animal death: grief. Marten's return to life reflects the Mi'kmaw belief that animals reincarnate, and will refuse to be caught if they are mistreated by previous hunters (Robinson 2014, 2016).

Being vegan has become a way I practice the values of my Mi'kmaw ancestors, such as respect for the personhood of other animals (Robinson, 2013) albeit differently from how my ancestors practiced them. The Mi'kmaq traditionally had a predominantly shellfish diet (Coates 2000) that they maintained through effective fishing technologies, supplemented by subsistence hunting and the gathering of fruits and vegetables. Colonial attempts to change our migratory lifestyle and tie us to the land included forcing us to practice agriculture, which was not a success.

Because hunting and fishing are part of the culture of many Indigenous nations, Settlers involved in the animal rights movement have tended to view Indigenous hunting as part of the systematic destruction of animal habitats and lives. Within such a framework, all hunting is part of a broader problem that has to do with how animals are treated as objects for sale and consumption. Indigenous communities tend to view the animal rights activism by Settlers as part of the ongoing genocide of Indigenous cultures and people, in the same category as residential schools, the destruction of our Indigenous languages, the criminalization of our cultures, the apprehending of our children by the state, the unlawful seizing of our lands, and environmental destruction for profit. In this way, the oppression of Indigenous people is part of a larger pattern of domination that includes oppressions such as speciesism.

The tendency for animal rights activists to focus on Indigenous hunting practices is somewhat bewildering if one values an economy of effort in which we focus our energies toward stopping those practices that have the broadest and most negative impact. For example, I was once invited to join some Settlers in a protest of the Indigenous deer hunt in what is now the Short Hills Provincial Park, part of the Haudenosaunee hunting territory recognized by treaty with the British in 1701 (Bolichowski, 2013). What was previously a vast wilderness has been reduced, by Settler expansion and development, into one of the most densely populated areas of Canada. In this way, Settlers get to keep their treaty rights to share the land while preventing the Haudenosaunee from exercising their treaty rights to subsistence hunting. The deer hunt in the Short Hills Park is a protest against colonialism and an exercise of treaty rights, while the Settler protest against the hunt unites animal rights activists with those who view Indigenous rights as outmoded and Indigenous people as a threat to humans and animals alike. Not a good scenario, from an Indigenous perspective.

I thought about how I would justify my participation to other Indigenous people. I could explain, I suppose, that I supported treaty rights (which I do), but not this particular exercise of them. Unfortunately, I know that failing to exercise Indigenous treaty rights has repeatedly resulted in their denial by Settlers, both here and in the US; so, the ability to exercise treaty rights is vital to securing justice for Indigenous people. I also thought about what my relationship of respect and kinship with other animals requires me to do when those siblings are in danger. I bought an orange poncho and an air horn, but I felt conflicted about using them.

The Indigenous deer hunt in Short Hills Provincial Park began in 2013 and kills about thirty-five deer each year (Animal Alliance of Canada, 2017; Walter, 2017). Service Ontario, the offices for governmental services in the province of Ontario, sells 190,000 deer hunting licenses annually (Paterson, 2017). Let's assume active hunters kill one deer per season. Let's assume further that half of the hunters don't kill any deer. That would still result in 95,000 deer deaths— nearly *a thousand times* the number in Short Hills.

Why weren't we protesting any of the 587 outlets of Service Ontario that sell hunting licenses? The outlets are accessible by transit, and they do the most damage; but they're a part of the normalized bureaucracy that makes up Settler Canada. I wondered if the protest of hunting in Short Hills might be an example of what Donna Baines terms the "flight to innocence," an effort to "elude the responsibility for changing oppressive relations by hiding behind some facet of their identity that locates them close to, or within, subordinated groups" (2002, p. 192). By identifying as protectors of the deer, activists continue Settler domination while avoiding guilt for the environmental devastation by Settler occupation that reduced deer to living in a Provincial Park.

The issue, it seems to me, is about Othering. It's easier to oppose the practices of a group that is already marked as different from one's own. This is where I find the concept of intersectionality to be particularly relevant.

## How Intersectionality Shines a Light on Speciesism

Kimberlé Crenshaw coined the term "intersectionality" to describe how gender and race oppressed women simultaneously (Crenshaw 1991, 1989), and Elizabeth Cole (2009) notes that the concept had been implicit in the work of many racialized scholars (Combahee River Collective, 1977; Davis 1981; Smith & Stewart, 1983; Lorde, 1983, 1984; Hurtado, 1989; Collins, 1990). Those of us with intersecting identities (e.g., vegan women), have different experiences than those in identity categories (vegan, women) separately.

Intersectional theory has helped me to understand how speciesism operates hand in glove with colonialism. Speciesism creates a hierarchy among humans based on our assumed similarity to, or distance from, other animals. I find this reflected in the way Indigenous people are treated: as if we are more like other animals than Settler are and, therefore, ill-equipped to make good decisions about our territories, our bodies, or our lives.

The doctrine of *terra nullius*, the idea that Settlers found "empty land" that could be claimed as their own (McMillan & Yellowhorn, 2009), reframes Indigenous people as part of the flora and fauna, enabling Settlers to justify treating us as a natural resource to be used, controlled, and managed instead of as people with a claim to the land on which we had lived (Gorman, 2016). Systems of oppression work together, like cogged wheels in a machine; oppressions work in tandem with colonialism, as well as with one another. White supremacy, for example, interlocks with Christian supremacy, serving as a divine justification for Settler domination and genocide by proposing that controlling our land is the "manifest destiny" of a divinely appointed Christian Settler population (Hill, 2017; Wilder 2014).

## Three Values Indigenous People share with Settler Vegans

Is it such a big deal if Setter vegans and Indigenous people don't get along? As someone who belongs to both groups, it's a problem for me because I hear colonial and racist comments when I spend time with Settler vegans (even those who are aware of and opposed to other oppressions, such as sexism or homophobia). For example, while riding through the Tonawanda Indian Reservation with some Settler activists, we saw a sign indicating that we were on unceded Indian land, which prompted a discussion about Indigenous hunting rights. The driver of the car explained that the only way he would support Indigenous hunting rights was if Indigenous people were forced to use bow and arrows we made ourselves. His argument is a common one that freezes Indigenous people in the past, without holding Settlers to the same standard. Settlers are not expected to live as they did when they signed specific treaties (e.g., in sod huts, or one-room houses), while Indigenous people are, because in a Settler worldview we represent the past and the primitive. Only expressions of Indigeneity that match these stereotypes are deemed "authentic" by Settlers.

The alienation of Settler activists from Indigenous people is also a problem if you're committed to the wellbeing of animals, as I am. It keeps Settlers and Indigenous people from working together on issues such as climate change, deforestation, and the environmental destruction caused by resource extraction and rampant consumerism. It prevents us from recognizing common ground on issues such as genetically modified and trademarked seeds versus wild or traditionally cultivated seeds. When I see Settler and Indigenous people working in solidarity— as they are doing in New Brunswick to oppose fracking— I notice that they are able to work together because of what they value as well as what they oppose.

While our cultural traditions are different, my experience of both Settler vegan and Indigenous communities helps me see the values we share in common. I'll examine three: *honesty*, *humility*, and *respect*. These are part of a larger set of values, sometimes called the Seven Grandparent Teachings. They are common to a number of Indigenous nations, and some have called them "the foundation of North American Indigenous belief" (Courchene, 2009). I learned these teachings in Anishinaabe territory, where the Seven Grandparent Teachings are *love*, *honesty*, *humility*, *respect*, *truth*, *wisdom*, and *bravery*. In Mi'kmaki, our teachings replace *bravery* with *patience*—perhaps because we've lived with colonialism for five hundred years, and have had to learn to be *very* patient.

Honesty, humility, and respect are values that relate most to the wellbeing of the other animals who share our territories, and they are values I see in Indigenous communities and practiced by Settler vegans in the animal rights movement.

## Honesty

By *honesty* I mean taking a clear and hard look at the decisions we make about the food we eat, the clothes we wear, and how those decisions impact us—physically, mentally, emotionally, and spiritually. I mean being honest about the power dynamics that shape and determine the agency we are able to exercise in the world.

I'm also talking about how our decisions impact the animals around us, and the environment on which we all depend. In short, I'm talking about being honest about how our choices impact "all our relations." If we're dedicated to living honestly, then we need to be aware of how a commitment to end speciesism is hollow if we aren't also committed to ending the interlocking oppressions that support and energize it, such as racism and colonialism.

## Humility

By *humility* I mean the ability to know yourself as part of the web of life, and not as the top of a food chain. Indigenous philosophy does not view human beings as the greatest life form, or as the top of a chain or pyramid. In fact, if we were to organize life hierarchically, we'd put humans at the bottom, because our philosophies frame the human as the most dependent of all creatures. More often, we view the human as part of an ecosystem in which every being has an important role. Similarly, Settler vegans who do animal rights activism show humility when they challenge speciesist views that frame humans as superior to other animals.

I'm told that in the Anishinaabe language the word for humility also means *compassion*. I grew up in the woods by a lake, and most of my interactions were with animals who depended on the lake — especially frogs, which who are a friendly and nonthreatening life form to a kid. One day, after a big rainstorm, my dad came into the house and said, "Hey, kids, I need your help. A frog laid a bunch of eggs in this puddle out back, and it's drying up now, and they're all going to die if we don't get them into the pond." For the next two hours, in the hot sun, we moved these gelatinous frog eggs and squirmy little tadpoles from their shrinking puddle into the pond. As we did so, I realized that, to my dad, the fragility of these animals mattered in the same way that our own fragility mattered. That experience revealed to me that "all my relations" means being humble enough to acknowledge our mutual vulnerability. When Indigenous people and Settler vegans unite in our humility we can work together to challenge the way the world denies that animals are our relations— that is, we can unite to challenge speciesism.

Faced with such a challenge, it can be tempting to cling to whatever privileges we might have; but, if intersectional theory is correct (and I think it is), then clinging to White supremacy—or Anglocentrism, or cultural supremacy, or Christian supremacy, or sexism, or heteronormativity— undermines our animal liberation goals by strengthening speciesism

## Respect

While we share this value, Setters and Indigenous peoples may demonstrate respect differently. One Mi'kmaw story tells of a family close to starvation during a harsh winter, who prayed for food. In response to these prayers, a moose appeared at their wigwam with a bargain. If they killed a moose only when in need, made tobacco offerings, and treated a moose's bones as sacred, then a moose would always return to feed the people. If they disrespected the moose, then they would leave and never return (Lefort, Paul, Johnson & Dennis 2014; Assembly of Nova Scotia Mi'kmaq Chiefs, 2009).

To show respect for the moose, the Mi'kmaq used as much of the animal's body as possible. The hide was used to make clothing, moccasins, and to wrap the exterior of our wigwams; tendons were used to create thread; bone and antlers were used to make needles, hunting tools, fasteners, and dice; and moose hair was used for embroidery. Once the bone marrow had been eaten, the Mi'kmaq would pound the bones to a powder and boil it to reap fat and produce a medicinal soup. Parts that cannot be used were returned to the creator via burial. Mi'kmaq hunters must also show respect for the moose by laying a circle of tobacco around the body and saying a prayer of gratitude. The hunter initiates a pipe ceremony to help release the animal's spirit, to ask forgiveness, and to let them know that the gift of their life is appreciated.

I sometimes encounter vegans who point to the Indigenous use of animal bodies as evidence of disrespect, as if there is one clear and obvious way to manifest respect. Settler vegans often assume that the only respectful response to animal death is to bury the body, treating it as they would a human body. I have heard Settler vegans critique the practice of making drums from animal skin, without understanding the spiritual or cultural meaning that is attached to the practice. "Would you do that to your grandmother?" I've had someone ask.

The appropriate treatment for a dead human, including one's grandmother, is determined culturally. In Settler cultures, mass graves were common among the poor, with individual burial being reserved for those who could afford it. Settlers have used the body parts of Indigenous people for a variety of purposes, with one Christian theology school in the state of Virginia displaying a book bound in the skin of an Indigenous person (Tinker, 2014). To the Mi'kmaq, using the body of a nonhuman animal sibling in its entirety is a requirement of respect. While teaching an Indigenous studies class, a Mi'kmaq-speaking student told me that there is no word for "garbage" in Mi'kmaq, and I find this very revealing of our cultural outlook.

Few sources describe the pre-contact burial practices of the Mi'kmaq, but one of our stories tells of a hunter with a spiritual connection to the moose, who transforms into a moose after his death in order to feed his sister (Rand 1893/2005). This suggests to me that my ancestors saw the difference between humans and other animals to be one of degree, and perhaps not one of kind (Robinson, 2014).

Most contemporary Mi'kmaq people don't hunt; we get our food from grocery stores, just like our Settler counterparts do. Nobody I know puts down an offering or holds a pipe ceremony when we buy food from the store; but the view that other animals are our siblings remains strong in our spirituality and our culture, and each Mi'kmaw person expresses their respect for that relationship differently.

In my case, I show my respect for my kinship ties with other animals by being vegan. I like to think Glooskap would understand that, and I'm sure Marten wouldn't mind.

## Cited Works

Animal Alliance of Canada (2017) *Deer hunt in Short Hills Provincial Park*:
https://www.animalalliance.ca/campaigns/other
-campaigns/deer-hunt-short-hills-provincial-
park/

Assembly of Nova Scotia Mi'kmaq Chiefs (2009*)* Tia'muwe'l Netuklimkewe'l, Unama'ki Moose Harvesting According to Netukuliml, Mi'kmaq Rights Initiative:
http://mikmaqrights.com/uploads/MooseGuideli
nes.pdf

Baines, D (2002) Storylines in Racialized Times: Racism and Anti-Racism in Toronto's Social Services, *British Journal of Social Work*, *32*(2): 185-199

Bolichowski, J (2013) Return of Deer Hunt Sparks Outcry, *The Standard*:
http://www.stcatharinesstandard.ca/2013/11/1
5/return-of-deer-hunt-sparks-outcry

Coates, K (2000) *The Marshall Decision and Native Rights* (Vol. 25), Montreal, QC: McGill-Queen's University Press

Cole, ER (2009) Intersectionality and research in psychology, *American Psychologist*, 64 (3): 170-80

Collins, PH (1990) *Black Feminist Thought: Knowledge, Consciousness, and The Politics of Empowerment*, New York, NY: Routledge

Collins, PH (1995) Symposium: on west and Fenstermaker's 'doing difference', *Gender & Society*, 9 (4): 491-513

Combahee River Collective (1977/1995): Combahee river collective statement in Guy-Sheftall, B. (Ed.), *Words of Fire: An Anthology of African American Feminist Thought* (pp. 232-40). New York, NY: New Press

Courchene, D (2009) Quoted in *the 7 Sacred Teachings*: http://the8thfire.org/teachings/

Crenshaw, KW (1989) Demarginalizing the Intersection of Race and Sex: A Black Feminist Critique of Antidiscrimination Doctrine, Feminist Theory and Antiracist Politics, *University of Chicago Legal Forum*, Chicago, 1: 139-67

Crenshaw, KW (1991) Mapping the margins: Intersectionality, identity politics, and violence against women of color. *Stanford Law Review*, 43 (6): 1241-1299

Davis, A (1981) *Women, Race, and Class*. New York, NY: Random House

Fish, J (2007) Navigating queer street: researching the intersections of lesbian, gay, bisexual and trans

(LGBT) identities in health research, *Sociological Research Online*, 13 (1): 12

Gorman, S (2016) Voices from the boundary line: The Australian Football League's Indigenous team of the century in *Indigenous People, Race Relations and Australian Sport* (pp. 100-111), CJ Hallinan and B Judd (Ed.) London, UK: Routledge

Fletcher Hill, J (2017) *The Sin of White Supremacy: Christianity, Racism, & Religious Diversity in America*, Ossining, NY: Orbis Books

Hurtado, A (1989) "Relating to privilege: Seduction and rejection in the subordination of white women and women of color," *Signs*, 14 (4): 833-855

Lefort, N, Paul, C, Johnson, E, and Dennis, C (2014) *Tiam: Mi'kmaq Ecological Knowledge: Moose in Unama'ki.* Unama'ki Institute of Natural Resources.
http://www.eecapacity.net/sites/default/files/fellows/docs/Moose%20in%20Unama'ki.pdf

Leland, CG (1884) *The Algonquin Legends of New England: Or, Myths and Folk Lore of the Micmac, Passamaquoddy, and Penobscot Tribes*, Boston, MA: Houghton, Mifflin

Lorde, A (1983) There is no hierarchy of oppressions, *Interracial Books for Children Bulletin*, 14 (3-4): 9

Lorde, A (1984) *Sister Outsider: Essays and Speeches*, Berkeley, CA: Crossing Press

Marahall, M (n.d.) *Mi'kmaw Seven Sacred Gifts of Life – Teachings of Elder Murdena Marshall*: http://www.integrativescience.ca/uploads/activities/Murdena-Seven-Sacred-Gifts.pdf

McMillan, AD, and Yellowhorn, E (2009) *First peoples in Canada*, Vancouver, BC: Douglas & McIntyre

Native American Legends: Nukumi and Fire (n.d.) First People: The Legends: http://www.firstpeople.us/FP-Html-Legends/Nukumi_And_Fire-Micmac.html

Paterson, S (2017) Ontario Federation of Anglers and Hunters ZONE "H" report for Bruce Peninsula Sportsman's Association: http://bpsportsmen.com/wp-content/uploads/2017/04/OFAH-March-April-2017-1.pdf

Rand, ST (1893/2005) *Legends of the Micmacs; Volume I*, West Orange, NJ: Invisible Books

Robinson, M (2013) Veganism and Mi'kmaq Legends, *Canadian Journal of Native Studies* 33 (1): 189-196

Robinson, M (2014) Animal Personhood in Mi'kmaq Perspective, *Societies* 4 (4): 672-688

Robinson, M (2016) Is the Moose Still My Brother If We Don't Eat Him? In: *Critical Perspectives on Veganism* (pp. 261-284), Castricano J & Simonsen RR (Ed.). New York, NY: Palgrave McMillan

Tinker, T (2014) "Redskin, Tanned Hide: A Book of Christian History Bound in the Flayed Skin of an American Indian: The Colonial Romance, Christian Denial and the Cleansing of a Christian School of Theology," *Journal of Race, Ethnicity, and Religion* 5(9), 1-43

Walter, K (2017) Short Hills Deer Hunt Cost $39,900, *St. Catherine's Standard*: http://www.stcatharinesstandard.ca/2017/05/0 3/short-hills-deer-hunt-cost-39900

Wilder, CS (2014) *Ebony and ivy: Race, slavery, and the troubled history of America's universities*, New York, NY: Bloomsbury Publishing USA

## *Move to Berkeley! and Other Follies*

### By Saryta Rodríguez

As a vegan of color, I have often encountered problematic strategies and rhetoric in the "animal rights community." I put that phrase in quotes because I employ it herein to refer to the more publicized, recognized organizations, networks and institutions in America working towards animal liberation. This by no means reflects the *entirety* of the animal rights community, which includes countless unsung individual heroes; organizations, networks and institutions with less visibility, often resulting from a decreased emphasis on fundraising and a refusal to ally themselves with more powerful organizations that are ethically questionable; and organizations, networks and institutions working towards animal liberation that do not obviously identify as such because their goals are broader-reaching and not exclusive to the protection of nonhumans.

Herein I will outline two detrimental pitfalls of the mainstream Animal Liberation Movement, in hopes that vegan activists will learn from these and develop a more cohesive, inclusive and compassionate strategy for inspiring non-vegans to make the difficult but necessary lifestyle changes that adhere to the Vegan Ethos requires.

### *I     A Decentralized Movement is a Healthy Movement*

I have written about the prejudice inherent in claiming that veganism is universally easy at *Reasonable Vegan*, in two essays entitled "Oppression Olympics and the Pitfalls of 'Animal Whites'" (2015) and "Exploding the Myth of the Moral Underclass." (2015). To sum up, to claim that veganism is unequivocally "easy" glosses over the very real plights faced by people every day that might prevent them from consistently adhering even to a plant-based diet, let alone to a full-on vegan lifestyle. Such people include, but are not limited to:

- the 14.5% of Americans currently living below the poverty line (United States Census Bureau 2014);
- those in prison, mental institutions, hospitals, or other places in which one does not have complete control over one's food options;
- those residing in food swamps (also known as food deserts (Wikipedia 2017), and
- those who live in extreme climates where produce is scarce or even non-existent.

There are, of course, myriad solutions to these problems. In my book, *Until Every Animal is Free*, (Rodriguez 2015) I highlight the need for more efficient and just food distribution as well as that for dropping the price point on hydroponic growing operations as two such solutions. Still, we must be honest about what is possible *right now* if we hope to inspire people to make a change *now* that might not be facilitated by such broad societal shifts until later.

As nonhuman animal advocacy groups go mainstream, receive checks from better-funded organizations and so become better funded themselves, they seem to be losing sight of the need to listen to their less fortunate counterparts even around the country (America), let alone the world. Some have claimed, for instance, that in order to be a truly effective advocate for nonhuman animals, you absolutely *must* move to an "activist hub," where there are already many activists such as yourself with whom you can team up to enact positive change (Hsiung 2015).

I totally get the strength-in-numbers mentality. I also recognize that not every nonhuman animal advocate has the means of moving even a few towns over, let alone across state lines or international borders.

Let's leave finances aside for a moment and talk family structure. If you are an advocate with school-aged children, moving them to a different town on the sole basis that there are more nonhuman advocates there— independent of choice of schools, the many friends your child or children has/have made in their hometown (and you have, too), the size of the home you can afford in the new city versus your current, and so forth— is unreasonable. It would be unreasonable of you to consider doing such a thing, and it would be unreasonable of any other activist to shame you for not doing so.

Now say you are the primary caregiver of an elderly person, like a grandparent. What if Grandma isn't physically *capable* of making the move? Does choosing to stay in Michigan with Grandma rather than move to Berkeley or San Francisco make you a bad activist?

Berkeley and San Francisco are two names tossed around by those who believe we must all cluster up in order to be effective. This is where the cost factor more obviously comes into play. While many nonhuman animal advocates have flocked to Berkeley (most, if not all, of whom are young, unmarried, and childless), I know of at least one— and incredibly strong, knowledgeable, talented writer, advocate and mother— who has been *pushed out* of Berkeley due to rising rents.

Should she just give up on her activism and hand the reigns over to those who can afford to stay there?

Other ways in which the mainstream nonhuman animal advocate community has failed to respect less-privileged activists include, but are not limited to:

- Suggesting that attending certain conferences inherently makes one more effective as an activist, when some can't even afford a ticket to those conferences, much less the affiliated round-trip flights;
- Suggesting that a "true" or "good" vegan will eat exclusively at establishments that are 100% vegan, when many vegans around the country and the world live in communities where there are no such establishments; and
- Suggesting that anyone who spends time in the company of someone who is eating animal byproducts is a "bad activist," when some don't have the luxury of choosing who they live with (which may include, say, an octogenarian who may well choke if you leave the room to spare yourself any discomfort or guilt). This inevitably leads to the exclusion of the impoverished, as

vegans are told not to sit with a homeless person who is eating a cheese sandwich— independent of what one might learn from that homeless person, or how they may yet be inspired to go vegan once they have regular access to food of any kind. The messaging here is, "I don't care if you starve, fellow human; if you violate my ethical code in order to survive by accepting a donated sandwich with animal products in it, then you are no longer worthy of my time, my company, or my compassion."

From a strategic standpoint, it is patently nonsensical to request all nonhuman animal advocates move to an urban activist hub, as this will draw activists away from places where nonhuman animal abuse is rampant, such as slaughterhouses and farms. These are the very sites where violence and oppression against nonhuman animals occur, and it is invaluable to our movement that we draw attention to these places and rally support for nonhumans among the locals. It is in towns where slaughterhouses and/or nonhuman animal farms reside that violence against nonhumans is perhaps the most normalized, even to the point of being revered as a means through which to financially support one's family.

Such areas need nonhuman animal advocates to stay: to raise their voices, their signs, their pens and keyboards loudly and proudly. Should nonhuman animal advocates flee them in favor of vegan echo chambers, the end result will be vegans preaching to the choir (as if we don't do enough of that already) while those who ignore the plight of nonhumans are left to do so in peace, surrounded by likeminded people. The victims' perspective will be erased from the very locales in which they are most victimized.

We will also become even less adept than we already are at reaching out to rural individuals, as members of our movement become increasingly reflective of the urban, educated, elitist mindset and alienated from the rural, less educated, more populist mindset. Vegans already living in rural areas without the means to move, meanwhile, may be less inclined to participate in a movement they perceive as having explicitly rejected them— or, at best, having minimized their contributions. There is one particular form of nonhuman animal advocacy that is in fact *hindered*, rather than improved upon, by living in activist hubs, and it is a crucial one: *sanctuary work*. Whether you run or volunteer at a larger sanctuary, such as Peaceful Prairie in Deer Trail, Colorado, or a microsanctuary, such as Triangle Chance for All in The Triangle, North Carolina, it is much harder to acquire space for both you and the nonhuman animals in your charge in a boomtown than it is in more rural areas. Moreover, larger nonhumans, such as cows, would most likely prefer to live in an open field than in a Bay Area backyard. After all, that's what this movement is supposed to be about: providing the best possible living situations for nonhumans, while protecting their basic liberties.

In this regard, you may be better equipped to serve the movement while living in Kansas or Arkansas than you would be if you moved to a boomtown and rented an apartment with six other people. It all depends on *how* you want to serve; the opportunities and possibilities vary widely.

Ignoring the realities many Americans face every day—such as caring for the elderly, living on a very limited budget, or caring for multiple children— while writing a prescription for activism is not only classist, but also indirectly racist. Statistically, people of color are more likely to care for an elderly relative than white people, including elders with special needs, such as those suffering from dementia (Torres 1999; Yarry, Stevens, & McCallum 2007)); have consistently larger families (Pew Research Center 2015), than white people (at least, as of 2013); and have an average household *wealth* (as opposed to income) that is *over half a million dollars lower* than that of white people ($571,000 less if they're Black; $558,000 less if they're Hispanic (Vega 2016)). Thus, proposed barriers to entry to the movement such as "You must live here" or "You must attend this" disproportionately exclude people of color.

The Animal Liberation Movement does not belong to any particular organization, town, or conference. It is a movement comprised of individuals from all walks of life, who come together to work towards a common goal. The more we alienate swaths of these individuals by making myopic, impractical demands, the longer it will take *all of us* to reach that goal.

## II  *Humans are Animals, Too*

A relatively recent definition I feel does a stellar job of explaining the *ethos* of veganism (while the above limits itself to the tenets of veganism—a rejection of the exploitation of animals in all of its various forms), is offered by Will Tuttle in his contribution to a collection of essays which he edited, entitled *Circles of Compassion* (2015):

*Even though we may be vegan in our outer lives and choices, veganism, we begin to realize, is far more than consumer choices, talking points, and animal rights campaigns. Veganism demands us to question absolutely everything in us that has been modeled by our cultural programming, and to bring our thoughts and deeds into alignment with a radically more inclusive ethic that calls for respect and kindness for all beings, including our apparent opponents. We see that veganism, as boundless inclusiveness, is the essence of all social justice movements, and that it is the antidote to what ails our world.*

In this definition, we see that veganism is about more than just abstaining from this or that product, or promoting this or that strategy for changing minds and challenging industry. It is an ethical standpoint that requires *boundless inclusiveness*— a respect for *all* sentient beings, as well as the planet on which these beings rely equally. There are those who identify publicly as vegan and yet, just as publicly, violate this crucial element of the Vegan Ethos. Examples include, but regrettably are not limited to, Gary Yourofsky, who showed a shocking level of disregard and even contempt for Palestinians, Black people and others in his video "Palestinians, Blacks and Other Hypocrites," (2015) and Freely the Banana Girl, who further demonstrated racism by asserting that the April 2015 earthquake that devastated Nepal was karma for the country's Gadhimai festival, during which millions of animals are slaughtered.

(This event, mind you, takes place once every five years, while billions of animals are slaughtered in the U.S. and other first-world countries annually for food, clothing and even mere sport.)

In the interest of mindfulness with respect to our activism, we could learn a valuable lesson from the Black Lives Matter movement, which has recently joined forces with Boycott Divestment and Sanctions (BDS, 2017), a group determined to boycott various Israeli companies operating in or otherwise profiting from illegal settlement on Palestinian land. We often speak in activist spaces about how to bring others to our cause, but we rarely, if ever, speak about how our cause is *already linked to other causes*. It is not a matter of persuading, say, a racial justice advocate that the lives of nonhuman animals are important, but rather for both the racial justice advocate and the animal liberationist to see the ways in which each of these struggles naturally depends on the success of the other. This is perhaps one of the most moving and spectacular coalition formations I have witnessed in many years, and I hope it will inspire many more. It is time we erased the borders that divide this injustice from that, and reject *all* injustice with equal vigor.

It is equally important to recall that very few people are "born vegan," i.e. raised vegan from birth. Most of us, regrettably, do contribute to nonhuman animal oppression for some portion of our lives. Campaigns that target individuals caught in the speciesist machine, demonizing them as inherently violent and malicious humans, are unfair at best and often, at worse, racially insensitive and bigoted. For instance, it is common to hear at slaughterhouse demonstrations various chants, and see various signs, intended to demonize factory farm workers— who, in America, are disproportionately of Mexican, Hispanic or Central-American descent. Such occurrences ignore the lived reality of these individuals, many of whom do not speak English, lack a formal education, and/or have families to support.

Does this mean all such individuals should get a pass to continue this line of work? No; but a more supportive, compassionate approach to encouraging a change in careers would ultimately be more effective, not to mention more just, than condemning them all outright as evildoers. One major contribution vegans of any color can make to empowering slaughterhouse workers to leave their jobs is to provide free or low-cost English language lessons at easily accessibly community centers, such as public libraries and parks. Basic career support, such as resume building and Excel spreadsheet proficiency, can also go a long way in helping someone who has never had another job before more confidently seek one.

The truth is, the vast majority of people employed at slaughterhouses don't actually *want* to be there. YouTube and mainstream nonhuman animal advocacy websites are rife with undercover footage of people punching and kicking nonhumans, as well as abusing them verbally; but these behaviors are not the norm. There are also myriad former slaughterhouse workers who do find their way out of the system and become valuable voices for nonhumans (Pippus 2016).

Even among those committing the most heinous acts

not required by their employer, there are those deserving of our empathy. Slaughterhouses are full of people with various mental illnesses— both people who come to the job with a preexisting illness and some who develop such illnesses (Lebwohl 2016) while employed at the slaughterhouse. These people don't need to be demonized, and doing so won't save nonhumans. What they need is professional psychiatric evaluation and intervention, not hateful rhetoric and social isolation.

In Ishmael Reed's *Blues City: A Walk in Oakland* (2003), Ishmael writes:

*According to a report from Pacifica's KPFA radio station, the police in Berkeley were cracking down on the homeless, while on January 14, 2003, Berkeley became the first city in California, and only the seventh in the nation, to issue a proclamation that farm animals have feelings and deserve to be protected, which gives the impression that Berkeley's city council cares more about the feelings of chickens than about those of the African-American veterans and others who are living on the streets of that same city.*

This is a prime example of both how unnecessary competition among struggles against oppression— Oppression Olympics— is fueled and how human members of oppressed communities may have come to feel excluded from and/or overlooked by the mainstream (Nonhuman) Animal Liberation Movement.

★★★★★

To me, the Vegan Ethos is not about creating a kum-ba-yah, everyone-loves-everyone society. Rather, it is about walking the path of least harm and respecting the right to autonomy of *all* sentient beings. Often, Oppression Olympics interferes with our commitment to respecting not only the individuals for whom we choose to campaign, but also those who campaign alongside us; those who oppose us; those watching from the sidelines, who have not yet chosen a position; and those who, independent of their ethical or intellectual inclinations, appear in direct opposition to us because of their employment status, what they are eating, what they are wearing, and so forth. The height of hypocrisy lies with those among us who seek to bring other humans aboard the Vegan Train while refusing to eat at table with them when all they can afford is a block of government-issued cheese, as well as those among us who stand self-righteously at the gates of slaughterhouses and declare that all "illegals" working there should be deported.

Moreover, the practice of tokenization— giving insincere optical prominence to vegans of color, female vegans, trans vegans and other marginalized vegans without fully accepting their feedback or heeding their advice— yields skepticism amongst members of those communities who want to save nonhuman animals from suffering and death, but who do not want to find themselves exploited as branding tools or fundraising fodder. Tokenization is also commonly deployed in order to dismiss and/or deflect criticism from marginalized communities. For instance, a mainstream nonhuman advocacy group may decide to utilize a tactic in spite of having multiple African-Americans voice their concerns about how the tactic falls short on the intersectionality front, simply because *one* African-American member of the group granted their approval.

As with any other social justice movement, in order for nonhuman animal liberation to be realized in even a national, let alone a global, scale, it is paramount that activists respect one another and support seemingly "other" justice movements as parts of the same whole. In reality, while different movements may focus on different populations, employ different tactics and have different historical roots, they are all united in the sense that they seek to create a fundamentally peaceful society.

This is not to say that incidents of violence can be fully eradicated from any society, or that it is possible to convince all individual actors worldwide— humans and nonhumans alike— to "like" one another. Anger, aggression and animosity are inherent in the animal condition, but there are ways in which we can promote our better selves while employing these seemingly negative qualities toward positive ends. Anger empowers us to speak out against injustice and cruelty. Aggression enables us to protect ourselves, our families and fellow inhabitants of Earth. Animosity creates an intellectual as well as an emotional internal conflict, which allows us an opportunity for personal growth as well as to achieve greater understanding of disparate points of view.

In summation, the two essential messages I hope nonhuman animal advocates derive from these pages are:

- That there are myriad ways in which one can contribute to the movement for nonhuman liberation, and that promoting only one of those ways is exclusionary (especially if that way comes with a price tag, like moving across state lines or attending expensive conferences); and

- That no nonhuman animal advocate should expect to be taken seriously when expounding the Vegan Ethos so long as they discriminate against, ostracize and/or demonize other humans.

## Cited Works:

Boycott, Divestment, and Sanctions (accessed 2017): http://bdslist.org/why/

Hsiung, W (2015) Should I Move…For the Animals? Lessons from Occupy Wall Street, *The Liberationist:* http://www.directactioneverywhere.com/theliberationist/2015/8/11/should-i-move-for-the-animals-what-occupy-wall-street-can-teach-animal-advocates

Lebwohl, Michael (2016) "A Call to Action: Psychological Harm in Slaughterhouse Workers," *Yale Global Health Review:* https://yaleglobalhealthreview.com/2016/01/25/a-call-to-action-psychological-harm-in-slaughterhouse-workers/

Pew Research Center (2015) *Households, by Family Size, Race and Ethnicity, 2013:*

http://www.pewhispanic.org/2016/04/19/statistical
-portrait-of-hispanics-in-the-united-states/ph_2015-
03_statistical-portrait-of-hispanics-in-the-united-
states-2013_current-40/

Pippus, A (2016) Meet the Former Slaughterhouse
Worker Who Became an Animal Rights Activist,
*Huffington Post*:
http://www.huffingtonpost.com/anna-
pippus/meet-the-former-
slaughter_b_10199262.html

Ratcliffe, Leanne (2015) Humans, *YouTube*:
https://www.youtube.com/watch?v=HaJgJ4Q8pV0

Reed, Ishmael (2003) *Blues City: A Walk in Oakland,*
Crown Publishing Group, New York

Rodríguez, S (2015) Oppression Olympics and the Pitfalls
of 'Animal Whites,' *Reasonable Vegan*:
http://rvgn.org/2015/07/31/oppression-olympics/

Rodríguez, S (2015) Exploding the Myth of the Moral
Underclass, *Reasonable Vegan*:
http://rvgn.org/2015/08/31/exploding-the-myth-of-
the-moral-underclass/

Rodríguez, S (2015) *Until Every Animal is Free,* Vegan
Publishers, Boston

Torres, S (1999) Barriers to Mental-Health Care Access
Faced by Hispanic Elderly in *Servicing Minority
Elders in the Twenty-First Century*, edited by Mary L.

Wykle and Amasa B. Ford: 200–218

Tuttle, W (2015) *Circles of Compassion.* Vegan Publishers, Boston

United States Census Bureau (2014) *Income, Poverty and Health Insurance Coverage in the United States: 2013:* https://www.census.gov/newsroom/press-releases/2014/cb14-169.html

Vega, T (2016) Blacks Will Take Hundreds of Years to Catch up to White Wealth, *CNN Money:* http://money.cnn.com/2016/08/09/news/economy/blacks-white-wealth-gap/

Wikipedia (accessed 2017) *Food Desert*: https://en.wikipedia.org/wiki/Food_desert

Yarry, S, Stevens, E K, and McCallum, T J (2007) Cultural Influences on Spousal Caregiving. *American Society on Aging,* 31 (3): 24–30

Yourofsky, G (2015) Blacks, Palestinians and Other Hypocrites, *YouTube:* https://www.youtube.com/watch?v=pqhUIns86cA

## *Sikhi, Ecofeminism, and Technology: Rambling Reflections of a Punjabi Intersectional Vegan Feminist*

### By Vinamarata "Winnie" Kaur

[TW: Rape, murder, and sexual assault references.]

I was born in a Sikh family in Punjab, India. While meat and seafood were luxuries that my father, paternal grandmother, and I could afford to indulge in only once a month, dairy was a staple commodity in our home, as was the case in several Punjabi households. My family got its daily supply of buffalo's and cow's milk at our doorstep every morning from a young boy who lived on a small, rural farm that provided his family with daily income. During my childhood, I did not really eat much meat beyond the chicken my father would get from the butcher once a month.

Dishes like *chicken tikka masala, chicken curry, chicken korma, saag paneer,* and *paneer makhani* are considered cultural identifiers of Punjabi-Indian cuisine and have found their way into almost all (North) Indian restaurants in the diaspora. Since food, both in its chemical and artistic forms, feeds our corporeal bodies, its cultural representations are interwoven with our interpretations of social relations. As a diasporic vegan-feminist, formerly physically-disabled and now temporarily able-bodied, Punjabi womxn of color based in the U.S., whose hybrid dis/identities are constantly in flux because of evolving sociopolitical climates, I have often felt stripped of my Punjabi identity because of my refusal to consume meat and dairy in a meat- and dairy-heavy culture.

I have also been shamed and verbally attacked by mainstream, "intersectional" yet speciesist feminist communities when I have suggested that our intersectional (Crenshaw 1991) frameworks should extend to Nonhuman animals so as to deconstruct phallogocentric binaries privileging a monolithic white, western, heteromasculinist, anthropocentrist discourse and its offspring of discriminatory -isms. Does consumption of animal-based "foods" not support capitalist empires (i.e. the billion-dollar meat and dairy industries that are often heavily subsidized in the U.S.) and deny personhood to the multitude (Others)? This denial was evident in my life through a forced sense of superiority inherent in consumption of meat and dairy as a marker of middle- and upper-class wealth—a notion that if we could afford Nonhuman animal flesh (like most people in the Global North have "evolved" to do), we were somehow better than people from lower socioeconomic backgrounds. As a child, I even remember starting to look down on my mother, a nutrition scholar and university professor that chose to be lacto-vegetarian after giving birth to me, because I saw her refusing to eat the meat she would cook for my father and me. I began to loathe myself for not being able to eat different kinds of meat often because of how expensive they were—I wanted to emulate a western lifestyle as projected by the media, and as such, became a victim of internalized oppression.

Such a false sense of superiority, forced upon us by media and societal assumptions and *trends*, benefits capitalist structures at the expense of Others and creates a skewed ideology of ethnocentric diets that are made up of slaughtered and constantly-suffering Othered bodies. Amidst all of this, our agency as subjects is reduced to that of an unconscientious consumer who becomes un/knowingly complicit in a cruel system of reproductive injustice and mass slaughter.

In the eyes of capitalism, the consumer exists simply to buy one product after another to generate a constantly supply of profits for the elite. Does it not become a feminist responsibility then to decolonize our bodies and minds by taking control of how and what we consume? Punjabi culture prides itself on hospitality and community service. Shouldn't it be thus a Punjabi ethic to decolonize its cuisine and lifestyle and establish a vegan manifesto that is emblematic of intersectional and equitable justice?

Sikhi is the fifth largest religion in the world (*SALDEF* 2017) that preaches egalitarianism. It is a reformed religion founded in parts of Punjab, India, that are now territorially a part of Pakistan. Nanak was the first Guru (teacher) of ten male-human avatars of the (gender-neutral) Divine Being. The origins of the religion date back to the early 1500s. One of the reasons Sikhi came into existence was to help Indian society get rid of inequities associated with Hindu practices of that time, such as *sati* (forced/voluntary widow-burning), female illiteracy, dowry, and *purdah* (use of face veils to protect womxn from the heterosexual male gaze). The ten Gurus condemned discrimination based on gender, caste, religion, and creed and taught people to embrace nature, conserve water, not to mistreat Other animals, and to believe in an interdependent ecosystem— which is why we never serve meat in *langar* halls (community kitchens) of any Gurudwara (holy place of worship for Sikhs). However, this compassionate practice of serving free lacto-vegetarian meals to all visitors (regardless of their background) is only confined to the religious space, thereby revealing a disconnect between several Sikh people's practices at the Gurudwaras and in their homes—where they continue to consume and serve meat.

By dismantling phallogocentric dichotomies and bodily boundaries that privilege (masculinist) anthropocentrism and its offspring—entanglements with speciesism, sexism, homophobia, ableism, interphobia, transphobia, and racism—I wish to see a reversal of what David Bohm (1980) calls "destruction of the balance of nature," such that recognition of complex personhood of dis/identities, rooted in ideals of interspecies justice, can be restored to shift the political, monolithic focus away from the human to the intersectional, hybrid, and often pluralistic posthuman. I'm interested in exploring how a (w)holistic understanding of discursive feminisms and ecologies can contribute to shifting perceptions of privileges and oppressions embedded in real-life immersive materialisms, which Donna Haraway (2003) refers to as "naturecultures." Considering theological (as well as thealogical) implications of our epistemological and ontological understandings of pluralistic identities, I wish to expand my theory of *cyborg thealogy*, which is a theory I designed a few years ago to connect our entangled digital, social, and spiritual selves and create spaces for sustenance for the Othered-identities, so as to also include Nonhuman animals. This cyborg thealogy will, at least theoretically, aim to alleviate these "non-normative," Othered classes of society (i.e. the queer, the womxn, the disabled, the person of color, among a plethora of "Others") of their "subhuman" species status, as projected through mainstream media, and transform them into empowered individual subjects that will act as agents of change for their communities. An application of my theory would then be to encourage proliferation of transnational and transdisciplinary discourses that will focus on achieving equity between non-normative and normative classes of society. The hope would be to move away from human-centered dialogues to deconstruct, construct, and reconstruct emergent notions of what it means to be human, companion/food, posthuman, cyborg, queer, non-queer, etc. in our materialist technoculture that often fails us through its non-recognition of plurality, hybridity, and multiplicity.

As it stands now, my theory of cyborg thealogy calls for interpellation of a compassionate politics rooted in vegan-ecofeminist principles. Technologies and media such as film, television, photography, and the Internet, have the potential to offer a technological and thea/ological space for us to confess our sorrows and "sins," as well as to share our joys and happiness. These technologies of confession offer us new solutions and ways to re-craft our lives, preparing us to face the "fiction" of social and environmental realities. Internet and films can thus be seen as "prosthetics" to our understanding of feminist "technologies of the self, which permit individuals to effect by their own means or with the help of others a certain number of operations on their own bodies and souls, thoughts, conduct, and way of being, so as to transform themselves in order to attain a certain state of happiness, purity, wisdom, perfection, or immortality" (Foucault 1988). Such technologies are both "dialogical" and "contemplative" and enable us to tell our stories and reflect upon our lives and their relations to Others through various mediums.

As much as these confessional technologies are potentially liberating, they are also unchained queer (i.e., out of the ordinary) monsters whose "myths are about transgressed boundaries, potent fusions, and dangerous possibilities which progressive people might explore as one part of needed political work" (Haraway 1991). Through my digital *darshan*— standing in the presence of a deity, beholding its image with one's own eyes— as a researcher and activist, witnessing the *bani,* or gospel, disseminating through these technologies, I consider myself evolving as an "insider-outsider." I feel like an "insider" in the sense that my family connection binds me to Sikhi, and "outsider" in the sense that while I realize technology's goddess-like prowess and acknowledge my Sikh roots, I can't completely separate myself from my agnostic identity. I have come to understand that technology holds over us a kind of self-disclosing and spiritually ameliorative power that could establish it as a professor of equity for those privileged enough to have access to it, such that it can be re-envisioned as an alternative *ashram,* i.e. a holy space, based on Sikhi's principle of *Ek Onkar* (oneness and equality for all). This egalitarian and monotheistic belief system allows global allies, whether tech-savvy Sikhs or not, to congregate in virtual affinity to understand how gender, race, ethnicity, species, and sexuality, among plethora of social factors, are manufactured as impediments to oppress the Others.

In 2014, Coca-Cola came under fire for perpetuating heterosexism and speciesism via its entry into the dairy industry through its Fairlife ad campaign. This campaign portrayed a number of white womxn models standing on a pile of milk, a weighing scale, and a swing and a Black womxn and another white womxn on a bicycle and a scooter. They were all clad in heels, sexualized through their visual depictions, dressed in white, flowy attires mimicking shrinking milk droplets— thus marketing extreme weight loss as a desirable side effect of their new products and perpetuating eating disorders and heterosexism (*India Today* 2014). This is in addition to its support of exploitation of baby calves and violation of the reproductive rights of female cows for their milk. This Fairlife campaign is just one of numerous incidents in commercial media in which womxn are treated as pieces of meat by animal agriculture industries that abuse Nonhuman animals through extreme suffering and devalue womxn by promoting eating disorders and hypersexualizing them. Black men are constantly shown in media to be brutes/beasts, thereby perpetuating the Angry Black Man stereotype. Men are often compared to pigs through the "boys will be boys" stereotype. Through the Jezebel stereotype, Black womxn's sexualities are often singularly equated to that of a Nonhuman animal by our racist and sex-negative cultures. In British India, Brown people like me were compared to dogs, with signs outside establishments that read, "Indians and Dogs Not Allowed." Gay and lesbian individuals are often portrayed as pedophilic predators by homophobic media. All of these comparisons that are meant to devalue anyone who's not a white, straight, man not only categorize the "deviants" as subhuman but also successfully establish an anthropocentric ideology that valorizes the human animal and disparages the Nonhuman animal as *something* unworthy of being instead of *someone* sentient who has a right to their life as much as any human animal.

As I reacquaint myself to my spiritual roots, I wish to see Sikhi's roots in ecofeminism and gender equality expand to a vegan politic that condemns not only media's mistreatment of womxn and people of color, but also consumption of meat, dairy, and eggs. Punjabi people like me should put an effort into establishing manifestos of their own to explore Punjabi-Indian ecofeminist and eco-thealogical associations of food and our connections with the Nonhuman world on a more holistic and spiritual level, grounding our scholarship in ideas of new-wave ecofeminist interspecies justice, so as to better recognize complex personhood of identities and connections between Sikhi and social justice. Resolving this culture-religion divide could potentially redefine our cultural kaleidoscope and reflect vegan-feminist principles that envision abuse-free farm and factory workers, healthier human animals, happier Nonhuman animals, and a prosperous planet.

However, let this not be a compassionate call that valorizes vegans while belittling everyone else because it is important we do not endorse *all* products that are labeled "vegan" or "cruelty-free." We need to make sure that the human animals who were involved in manufacture and distribution of those products were paid living wages and treated fairly. For example, we can't be eating "cruelty-free" chocolate covered in the blood and sweat of children of color from African countries (Food Empowerment Project 2017) while ignoring that most people (of color) who work in slaughterhouses also suffer from extreme trauma and PTSD (McWilliams 2012). It is for these interconnecting reasons that I am not just a vegan or a feminist, but an intersectional vegan ecofeminist. I do not support the colonialism and speciesism of mainstream feminist movements, nor do I endorse the sizeism, neoliberalism, classism, sexism, and racism of mainstream white-veganism movements. Intersectional feminism that doesn't address speciesism (and its detrimental effects on people and Other sentient beings) is exclusive and another form of elitist, white feminism, thereby making it anti-intersectional. Analyzing speciesism allows us to view how crooked, selective, and discriminatory our moral compasses are when we continue to voice our concerns against abuse of specific kind of marginalized bodies while ignoring the pain of Others.

I realize I occupy this liminal space of in-between-ness between vegan and feminist communities. While mainstream (white) feminism supports anthropogenic exploitation of Nonhuman animals and continues to silence subaltern voices, especially those of womxn of color like me and of Other species, mainstream veganism fails to address the class divide and inherent racial connections that affect many human animals' access to (w)holistic, (mostly) cruelty-free nutrition in food deserts, for example. While Nonhuman animal rights advocates and mainstream feminists practice speciesism by voicing their concerns against exploitation of certain animals (mostly human animals and companion species, such as dogs and cats), they ignore the rights and personhood of all Other animals (the animals we breed, consume, use, exploit, hunt, wear, and kill for our greed).

Several environmentalists, including large non-profit organizations, suggest driving hybrids or using public transportation, taking shorter showers, composting and recycling, washing our clothes on cold water cycles, etc., but they often shy away from the advice that people need to eliminate their consumption of Nonhuman animal byproducts to conserve our resources and slow the rate of climate change. It comes as a surprise to me that we're fighting against similar forms of interconnected oppressions over and over again, and the resistance we face from those whose ideologies we challenge is monumental. The Supreme Court ruling on monogamous same-sex marriage in 2015 suggests that we've tried recently as a nation to eliminate at least one of those forms of oppressions (Obergefell v. Hodges). Considering we're all part of the same ecosystem, we need to nurture our Earth so that it can love us back. Nonhuman animal rights are as important as any human animal rights issues, for everyone experiences suffering and pain in unique ways. It's counterproductive to compare one form of oppression with another (Lorde 1983). Even the new Papal Encyclical, issued by Pope Francis on 24 May 2015, on environment and human ecology seeks to establish connections between caring for the Earth and caring for marginalized communities.

As I end my raw, ruminating reflections, I'd like to note here that in order to develop my intersectional ecofeminist theory of cyborg thealogy rooted in interspecies justice (that dismantles the discriminatory concepts of hierarchy and privilege), I've been inspired by a lot of important works, some of which are Amie Breeze Harper's *Sistah Vegan* (2010), Maria Mies and Vandana Shiva's *Ecofeminism* (2014), *Goodbye Gauley Mountain* (2013), and *Cowspiracy* (2014). *Cowspiracy* also drew my attention to *World Watch*'s groundbreaking study that cited animal agriculture and livestock rearing to account for 51% of the annual worldwide greenhouse gas emissions (Goodland and Anhang 2009). Indulging in anthropogenic privileges with a colonial mindset that favors human animals over Other species and believing in a Western, "God"-given right to dominate and domesticate Other species contributes to validation of various forms of discriminations in society, may they be cis-heterosexism, racism, or speciesism. To regard Nonhuman animals and Oppressed humans as subhuman allows the master to control, murder, torture, incarcerate, rape, assault, and reign over these marginalized Other(s). Moving away from western notions of dualisms and practices and applying principles of *Ek Onkar* allow room for cyborg thealogy and ecofeminism within Sikhi to pave way for an inclusive intersectional philosophy of justice that can be used by people of all faiths, or even the deviant ecosexual misfits like me who doubt the existence of God but happily embrace nature as goddess and lover, dreaming of future plant-based *langars* and rejoicing to the fragrant smells of *saag tofu* and *chick'n tikka masala*!

## Cited Works

Bohm, D (1980) *Wholeness and the Implicate Order*: http://www.gci.org.uk/Documents/DavidBohm-WholenessAndTheImplicateOrder.pdf

*Cowspiracy* (2014): http://www.cowspiracy.com

Crenshaw, K (1991) Mapping the Margins: Intersectionality, Identity Politics, and Violence Against Women of Color, *Stanford Law Review*, 43(6): 1241-1299

Food Empowerment Project (2017) *F.E.P.'s Chocolate List*: http://www.foodispower.org/chocolate-list/

Foucault, M (1988) *Technologies of the Self*, L. Martin, H. Gutman, & P. Hutton: http://www.umass.edu/umpress/title/technologies-self

*Goodbye Gauley Mountain* (2013):
    http://goodbyegauleymountain.org

Goodland, R and Anhang, J (2009) *Livestock and Climate Change*:
    http://www.worldwatch.org/files/pdf/Livestock%20and%20Climate%20Change.pdf


Haraway, D (2003) *The Companion Species Manifesto: Dogs, People, and Significant Otherness*:
    http://press.uchicago.edu/ucp/books/book/distributed/C/bo3645022.html

Haraway, D (1991) *Simians, Cyborgs and Women: The Reinvention of Nature*, 149-181

Harper, A B (2010) *Sistah Vegan: Black Female Vegans Speak on Food, Identity, Health, and Society*:
    http://www.sistahvegan.com/sistah-vegan-anthology/

*India Today* (2014) Can sex sell milk? Coca Cola thinks so with its new campaign:
    http://indiatoday.intoday.in/story/coca-colas-premium-milk-fairlife-gets-off-on-wrong-start-with-sexist-ads/1/404732.html

Lorde, A (1983) *There is No Hierarchy of Oppressions*. In Leonore Gordon's *Homophobia and Education*, Interracial Books for Children Bulletin, 14 (3)

McWilliams, J (2012) *PTSD in the Slaughterhouse*:

https://www.texasobserver.org/ptsd-in-the-slaughterhouse/

Mies, M and Shiva, V (2014) *Ecofeminism*:
http://press.uchicago.edu/ucp/books/book/distributed/E/bo20842312.html

Obergefell v. Hodges (2015):
https://www.supremecourt.gov/opinions/14pdf/14-556_3204.pdf

Pope Francis (2015) Encyclical Letter:
http://w2.vatican.va/content/francesco/en/encyclicals/documents/papa-francesco_20150524_enciclica-laudato-si.html

Sikh American Legal Defense and Education Fund (2017)
*Who Are Sikh Americans*: http://saldef.org/who-are-sikh-americans/

# Interviews

## *Exploring Vegan Spirituality: An Interview with Six South Asian Vegan Womxn*

## By Vinamarata "Winnie" Kaur, Bipasha Ahmed, Deepta Rao, Meenal Upadhyay, Ankita Yadav, and Laila Kassam

This collaborative interview highlights the reflections of six womxn who grew up in diverse South Asian households and embraced veganism while coming to terms with their inner spiritualities. This piece has been influenced by these womxn's experiences living in India, England, Scotland, and the United States.

*****

Being vegan, we share a deep regard for nonhuman animal rights and consider our shared passion for caring for the plight of nonhuman animals to be a major influential factor in guiding our food and lifestyle choices. As feminist womxn of color, we understand the intersectionality of oppressions (cf. Kimberlé Crenshaw's "Mapping the Margins," 1991) that intertwine the struggles of (hetero)sexism, racism, classism, casteism, colorism, speciesism, sizeism, interphobia, transphobia, and xenophobia (among others). We approach this piece from the perspective of self-defined, food-centric spirituality that emphasizes wholeness in nourishing the body as well as the mind without deliberate harm to other sentient beings.

Vegan spirituality should not be a privilege but an accessible, non-exploitative way for us to experience connections to ourselves and to nature. It should be a socially-conscientious practice that reflects not only on ourselves but also on our direct and indirect experiences with Others: people from different cultures, as well as the many nonhuman sentient beings in our shared ecosystem.

Although our veganism extends beyond caring for nonhuman animals solely used in food, diet plays a large role in our personal, political, social, economic, and spiritual lives. Given that the menus of South Asian cuisines are extremely diverse, with many delicacies being already vegan (or easily veganized) and often focusing on simple, wholesome ingredients such as vegetables, lentils, legumes, spices, and grains as the main ingredients, there are several reasons for us to advocate for plant-based, decolonized diets.

Though we are not all avid yoga practitioners today, we practice spirituality in our unique ways. A discourse on South Asian vegan spirituality won't necessarily be complete without also addressing the inherent cultural colonization infiltrating several "yoga" spaces, especially in the Global North. Thus, we will also explore our perspectives on being witnesses to the cultural appropriation and exoticization of South Asian symbols and languages to sell yoga (which, for many, is a religious and/or spiritual practice rooted in cultural and historical traditions of India and East Africa, and is only one of several forms of meditation practices) as a new fitness trend without regard to feelings, experiences, and spiritual sentiments of people with South Asian roots.

Since not all of us have connections to East Africa, we do not feel adequately positioned to discuss at length the roots of Kemetic yoga. Thus, we dedicate Question Three below to "yogic" spaces and practices that are most familiar to us. In answering this question, we attempt to make sense of some of our individual frustrations and give advice on decolonizing yoga and our diets.

Lastly, we want to acknowledge the fact that, while we want this collaborative piece to represent the diverse and transnational voices of South Asian vegan womxn, all of us, albeit coincidentally, come from various interdisciplinary backgrounds and have had certain class and education privileges that have contributed to our veganic "spiritual" awakenings.

**1. Growing up in a South Asian household, how did you and your family and friends practice meditation (if applicable)? What do these spiritual practices mean to you as a vegan womxn with South Asian roots?**

**Winnie:** The homes in which I was raised— in Punjab, India— were comprised of my paternal grandparents, Mom, Dad, my brother, me, and our different animal companions through time. My grandpa was my role model—a compassionate vegetarian and my greatest source of inspiration to pursue higher education. After finishing her doctorate in nutrition and giving birth to me, my mom had an epiphany and decided to stop eating meat and eggs. It was then only my dad (who has now been an egg-free vegetarian for almost a decade), my late paternal grandma, my brother (who is now slowly learning to appreciate plant-based cuisines), and I who "indulged" in meat and seafood— once in a while, when we could afford to— during my childhood.

My grandparents listened to *shabads* and *kirtan* (religious musical narrations) on the radio and television every morning and attended the local Gurudwara (holy place of worship for Sikhs) for community prayers. My grandma usually performed the morning prayer service at home, while my mom performed the evening prayers. At times, I would join my grandparents and mother in these prayers. My maternal grandparents, who lived in another city in Punjab, were also (egg-free) vegetarians. At my Catholic school, we were required to perform morning and afternoon prayers and sing hymns that praised Jesus and Mother Mary. During my dance, music, and physical education classes, we had to recite patriotic melodies and praise the Christian and Hindu gods and goddesses through musical performances. At times, these classes involved yoga sessions. Thankfully, these yoga classes didn't preach cultic asceticism or celibacy (both isolated practices that Sikhi condemns), but were a way for us to meditate and engage in something beyond the books. Dance, yoga, and prayers (in praise of the nation, Sikh Gurus, Jesus, Mother Mary, Hindu deities, or nature) thus became my avenues for meditation.

As I grew up, I separated myself from the nationalist ideologies that were forced upon me through media and daily patriotic rituals at school, and my multifaceted religious identities adopted a globally-inspired translocal mindset. I started meditating through hip-hop* and dance. By embracing vegan and feminist reading and viewing materials, I attempted to feed my soul with pro-intersectional energy. In cooking Punjabi and fusion meals, I started practicing mindful meditation through decolonization of my diet by sticking to plant-based ingredients. All of these experiences, past and new, have enabled me, as a Punjabi-NRI (nonresident Indian, permanent resident-U.S. American) womxn of color, to appreciate feminist and queer theologies; thrive in my current vegan feminist lifestyle (devoted to Mother-Lover Nature as my spiritual goddess) that prioritizes intersectional*, equitable justice for all (human or nonhuman); and practice meditation through deep breaths and walks in nature with my special needs canine companion (who is also vegan, primarily because of our family's ethics and secondarily because of his animal protein allergies, which aggravate his megaesophagus— a debilitating disease).

*I attribute my intersectional and hip-hop meditative awakenings to Black scholars, artists, and activists.

**Bipasha:** I grew up as a Bengali Muslim in the U.K. As such, I don't feel that I have ever explicitly practiced meditation. I was, however, taught *Namaaz* (the physical and spiritual ritual for performing Islamic prayers) as a child. Having had many conversations with Indian and Bengali friends since, I can now see that there is much overlap between Muslim and Hindu methods of prayer and meditation (including yoga). I have developed an understanding of these practices within the historical and social context of myriad Indian cultures and how, arguably, these overlaps are inevitable. As a child, I had never conceptualized my experiences of *Namaaz* in this way.

I have also gained some understanding of the historical

animosity between Hindus and Muslims in the subcontinent, particularly in the Bengal region. For many people, Islamic spirituality was deliberately defined as different from Hinduism, and I certainly saw these prejudices reflected in the views of my extended family. This was probably at least part of the reason than I had not recognized the overlaps in my youth. Despite these retrospective reflections, I do not consider meditation as part of my experience growing up in a South Asian household.

By the time I had become an adult, I no longer followed any religious practice. I do have enormous respect for and interest in Islam and the political history of Muslim people. I still feel a part of that community, which is important to me— especially in the face of current Islamophobia. However, I do not feel that spirituality, as most people understand it, is a part of my experience. Despite my rejection of religion as an adult, I do feel that my upbringing as a Muslim has an effect on how I understand and experience my veganism in some respects.

For example, although we know there has been a long and strong tradition of vegetarianism in South Asia, for my family and many Bengali Muslim friends, my vegetarianism and eventual veganism have been seen as problematic. This is partly because of how vegetarianism is perceived as associated with Hinduism, but also because meat-eating is considered by many to be an integral part of Muslim practice (although there are many Muslims, including those that identify as Muslim vegans and vegetarians, who have different views and interpretations of Islamic practices related to animals).

Outside of religion, I feel very strongly about my South Asian roots. For example, it shapes my identity as a second-generation Bengali womxn living in the West. It connects me to Others from similar backgrounds and, as such, I feel a strong sense of solidarity with Other South Asians and people of color, particularly in the face of racism. I have children now, and it has become especially important to me that they are aware of their heritage now that we live in the West. Having been involved in various forms of anti-racist and feminist activism most of my adult life, I see veganism as part of an intersectional approach to my political activism. I feel very strongly about my veganism, but for me, the decision to avoid relying on and using animals is very much an ethical, political stance, rather than a spiritual one. In other words, my veganism is predominantly about social justice, but it has been important to me to be able to also understand it as part of my identity as a South Asian womxn from a Muslim background.

**Deepta:** I come from a Hindu Brahmin family and was born and raised in India. I lived in the capital city of New Delhi during my childhood and later moved to Bangalore in South India during my teenage years. My earliest memories include sitting beside my mother as she would light the lamps at our home altar and my father's clear chanting of the vedic *shlokas* (couplets) would echo through the room. I have seen my parents practice Hinduism in all its glory—from a simple daily *pooja* (prayer) to celebrating big festivals like *Diwali* in all its pomp; from going through a round of the *japa-mala* (prayer beads) to elaborate rituals of a *hawan* (oblations to the fire); from visiting temples a stone's throw away to climbing a treacherously steep hill far from home, and from discussing everyday moral stories of folklore in vernacular to a month-long immersion in sacred texts scripted in the language of the Gods—*Sanskrit*.

The rituals and practices of Hinduism provide an opportunity for every caliber of our consciousness to engage the sense organs and mind to seek the divine. I recall special *pooja* days of decorating the front of my home in a traditional *rangoli* (artful floor decoration) as *bhajans* (devotional songs) would play on the radio, and the smell of sweet *kheer* (a dessert usually made out of cow's milk) wafted into my nostrils. I recall the little fights my brother and I would have over who got a chance to ring the *ghanti* (bell) or offer flowers to the deities. We would definitely fight over who got the bowl with a tad bit larger share of the *kheer*—now *prasad* (*kheer* offered to the divine turned into a blessing). My parents encouraged me to learn the chants and the procedure of the rituals. They did not compel me, but instead led by example. "It gives you peace of mind," my mother would tell me. We did not sit in *padmasana* (lotus pose) with our fingers in *dhyan mudra* (meditative finger gesture) to find that peace. In my parental home, the deep immersion in any God-/Goddess-centric activity was a meditation in itself. I continued on this path, as it resonated deeply within me. Eventually, I did "meditate" in a yoga class.

My South Asian origins in a religion that places such strong emphasis on peaceful coexistence led me to embrace veganism. In veganism, I find the same peace that my mother found in her daily prayers. In veganism, I find the same peace that my religion teaches.

**Meenal:** I grew up, for the most part, with my very conservative extended North Indian Brahmin family— in which, to this present day, married womxn cover their faces and girls don't laugh out loud in the presence of elders. Those were deeply religious surroundings, with strict practices for cooking, eating, washing, and worshipping; but my parents were very liberal for their time, and my mom always encouraged me to ask the "whys."

Surprisingly, my granny always had answers to those "whys." Why do we need to eat before sunset? Why can't I be served with the rest when I am menstruating? Why should I not pluck flowers at certain times? Why do you not allow me to watch an eclipse? She always had answers (although ones that were a bit irrelevant to the current times). Within this conflicting upbringing of fierce religiousness and extreme liberal views, I found that my calling was more spiritual and less religious. Instead of practicing the "right way to worship" an entity confined to a lifeless idol, I formed a deep bond with an inner voice that was rational. I found great peace during the elaborate evening *poojas,* because that was the time I could dissociate myself from everything and focus my senses on the lighted *deepak* (lamp), the smell of fresh flowers, and the soul-elevating music with sounds of the bell.

Those were my first encounters with meditation, although I did not formally know it as that then. It helped me feel a connection with everything around me—a sense of belonging everywhere and responsibility for all of my actions. At that initial stage, I felt being a vegetarian was my contribution to making the world a better place.

Moving to the U.K. and meeting some vegan groups opened up a whole new world for me; it was sort of a definitive answer to all of the doubts I had. I now feel connected to everything in the world. I realize that a seemingly simple thing like consuming chocolate can have an oppressive ripple effect on humans, nonhuman animals, and the environment.

## 2. How did you first get involved in veganism, and how do you perceive it to be connected to spirituality and/or social justice?

**Winnie:** A few years ago, in late 2012, I started exploring pescetarianism (and later, vegetarianism) for mostly health reasons— so as to include more vegetables and greens in my diet. I started cooking healthier meals at home. Soon after, having developed lactose intolerance and slightly elevated cholesterol levels, I started avoiding dairy and eggs. Then it was time to choose exam areas for my comprehensive doctoral exams, and I wanted to study something meaningful that promoted healthy living and sustainability, so I chose environmental literature. Having chosen feminist and queer theories and media studies as my other areas of specialization, I built upon my existing body of knowledge to establish stronger connections among feminism, environmentalism, and veganism. I could no longer call myself a feminist or an environmentalist if I continued participating in a culture that exploited womxn, people of color, and nonhuman animals. I began by eating fully vegan at home and vegetarian at restaurants (where fully vegan was often not a possibility) with the aim that I would slowly start ordering vegan at restaurants as well. This transition happened to coincide with meeting my spouse in 2014. When I first started dating him, I often saw him ordering plant-based at non-vegan restaurants and felt the urge to follow suit. I'd already decided at that point that I could not romantically be with anyone long-term who consumed animal products and alcohol (and my partner shared the same beliefs), so being with him provided the push I needed to fully embrace a vegan lifestyle, both within and outside of my home.

As I adopted a vegan-feminist lifestyle, I started researching connections between diet and spirituality. I started going to the local Gurudwara (the religious place of worship for Sikhs) and bringing my friends from other faiths along so they could enjoy a nice free meal while learning more about the Sikh community in the U.S. Despite several requests, my local Gurudwara in the Greater Cincinnati region of Ohio refused to omit dairy from their meals, leaving rice the only option at most *langars* (community-cooked, egg-free vegetarian meals prepared by volunteers and available for free to all visitors, regardless of their socioeconomic or religious backgrounds), which led me and my friends to eventually stop going to the Gurudwara.

Since Gurudwaras only serve egg-free vegetarian *langars* (and forbid alcohol on their premises), and because I grew up in a Sikh family, my latest project involves researching Gurus' teachings in relation to ecosystems, animal suffering, and diet, through my interpretations of the scriptures in the *Guru Granth Sahib* (holy book for Sikhs). Gurudwaras should not exclude vegans because the entire purpose of *langars* is *seva* (selfless service) for all, based on the concepts of community welfare, inclusiveness, and equity. Given that several religious scriptures in Sikhi, Hinduism, Christianity, Islam, Judaism, Buddhism, and Jainism (and, I'm sure, other faiths as well) point to a reduction in harming others (just as veganism also promotes causing as minimum of a harm as possible to other sentient beings), I consider veganism, social justice, and spirituality to be closely connected— for even the agnostic, nature-worshipping folks, like me.

**Bipasha:** I became vegetarian about twenty-seven years ago. I gave up eating meat first, but I struggled with giving up fish. I think this was because being of Bengali origin, we ate a lot of fish, so it took me a couple of years longer to stop than it did to stop eating land meat. My reasons for becoming vegetarian back then are almost identical to my reasons for being vegan now. I previously described how spirituality is not a major feature of my experience, but being concerned for social justice always has been. I do not want to rely on other animals in any way as doing so, to me, is wrong and do not want to be supportive of any practices that oppress either humans or nonhumans. Thus, I recognize that the animal agriculture industry has enormous detrimental effects on the planet for both people and the environment as a cause of climate change. The same industry directly impacts vulnerable communities through oppressive practices, causing further inequalities in access to food and food choices of already exploited and otherized communities.

Before I became vegan, as with many vegetarians I knew at the time, I seemed to have a bit of a block with respect to veganism. I knew that I shared the same political and ethical motivations for being vegetarian as many vegans, and thus, deep down knew that I "should" be vegan. However, at the time, I genuinely felt that being vegetarian was "good enough," and I could somehow be forgiven for still eating dairy and eggs. I tried several times to be vegan, and, after I got married, both my partner and I would intermittently attempt veganism; but we never managed more than a few weeks at a time.

Fast forward a number of years. I had children, who my partner and I raised vegetarian. We always tried to explain to them why we were vegetarian and answered any questions they had, so they were always very clear about our ethical and political commitments to vegetarianism. Then one day, my eldest daughter (who was eleven years old at the time) asked us, "If we are vegetarian for the reasons we say we are, then why aren't we vegan?" We admitted that we should be, but we had just not managed it yet. She then stated that she wanted to become vegan.

My daughter became vegan that day. She never hesitated, never looked back, and never at any point "fell off the wagon." My partner and I both felt that we had no excuse after that. We both took a little longer to be as confident as our daughter, but that was seven years ago now.

I see my veganism as activism. I have been involved in political activism most of my life. This is also reflected in my work as an academic and as a trustee for a South Asian women's domestic violence refuge for over 15 years. I see veganism as a form of social justice. Having said that, as a South Asian Bengali womxn who was brought up Muslim, I often engage in discussions about how veganism does not fit in with certain ideas about religious practices. Many of my religious friends and family know that I am no longer religious, and view this with great disappointment. They see my veganism as further evidence of my "moving away from God." Their understanding is that animals are God-given for humans to utilize. This has always been a difficult discussion for me to engage in, and has often felt futile. These difficult conversations led me to connecting with vegan Muslims, mainly on social media, which has allowed me to see different possibilities for engaging friends and family in debates about my veganism.

For example, I am beginning to develop an understanding about spirituality and veganism even though I do not consider myself as spiritual. Despite now feeling that I have access to arguments and ideas about why veganism can be seen as part of Islamic practices rather than in contradiction to it, I still feel that a major issue for many of my Bengali Muslim friends and family is that they will never accept that utilization of nonhuman animals for human benefit is a problem. In addition, I still have many family members who live in poverty in Bangladesh, and I would, of course, feel uncomfortable imposing my views about food choices on them. I am also acutely aware of the irony that being able to choose veganism can be perceived as a privilege, and many feel they do not have the luxury to be able to choose not to eat meat.

**Ankita:** I must have been less than 5 years of age when my interaction and care for nonhuman animals around me began. My engagement with veganism happened as a result— as a link further in a chain reaction. Recalling from my school lessons, when I was taught the names of the offspring of the animals, I used to ask my parents, "Those people mentioned that they are eating chicken, but chicken means that bird who is the child of the hen, right? How can they eat a bird? You mean they killed them? They must have cried when they died, right?" I often used to imagine the plight and pain of having a knife run across my throat and then think of the chickens. According to me, that is how they were killed. I was unaware of the processes of the factory farms. My parents spent a long time pulling me out of a semi-depressive mode after that and instilling in me the motivation to act into which that depression should translate. That is how I have stayed a vegetarian all my life, by choice. As I got older and learned about veganism, it became a part of my life. Veganism for me is a very simple progression of my love for animals.

**Laila:** When I started to look into spirituality, I began to see how conditioned we are— by society, family, inherited cultural beliefs, our education systems, the mass media, and so many other influences. I also realized how little time I spent in the present moment and how many of my thoughts and behaviors were habitual and unconscious. I decided to make a concerted effort to be more present, conscious, and mindful, and to live nonviolently. I started to practice meditation and soon realized that I could not eat animal flesh mindfully. I started to see "steaks" and "burgers" for what they were—the corpses of tortured animals. I became vegetarian in 2010. Sometime later, I began educating myself about the dairy and egg industries. In 2013, I finally realized how morally inconsistent my vegetarianism was and became vegan. There was no specific "aha" moment that I can remember, and no particular Facebook post that flicked the switch. It was more of an increasing realization that if I truly wanted to live consciously and with integrity, I needed to align my actions with my beliefs that it is wrong to cause unnecessary harm to other animals.

In this respect, my journey to veganism came out of a personal spiritual search. Most spiritual traditions believe in respecting all life, nonviolence, and treating others as you would like to be treated, but these beliefs are not exclusively "spiritual." Species is no more a relevant criteria than are race, sex, class, or ability to exclude others from the moral community. To me, veganism, anti-speciesism, and animal rights are fundamental matters of social justice.

In the last few years, I have also begun to realize how interconnected animal exploitation, human oppression, and environmental destruction are and how the mentality required to oppress, exploit, and dominate other animals is the same mentality that allows us to oppress, exploit, and dominate humans and destroy our planet. Reading *The World Peace Diet* by Will Tuttle and *Animal Rights Human Rights: Entanglements of Oppression and Liberation* by David Nibert opened my eyes to how the oppressions of humans and of other animals are deeply entangled—how the oppression of one devalued group often compounds that of other devalued groups, and how these entanglements are driven by economic motivations, especially under corporate capitalism. This kind of understanding is crucial for the overall struggle for social justice and total liberation.

## 3. What have been your experiences in "yoga" spaces (if applicable)?

**Winnie:** Besides communally practicing yoga in North India during my childhood, my experiences with "yoga" spaces in the U.S. have been limited. I have only taken a few hot "yoga" classes at a local studio in Midwestern Ohio and choose to instead practice meditation at home while listening to relaxing sounds. However, I'm aware of several "yoga" classes being offered at schools around me as part of their fitness activities. Through my online and offline ethnographic research, I have found most "yoga" spaces to be more culturally-appropriative and less racially-inclusive. I also find many of these spaces guilty of body-shaming. I would like such "yogic" spaces to embrace yoga's roots in Hinduism, Buddhism, Jainism, and/or Kimet civilizations and be culturally-appreciative spaces for people of all sizes and races. One of my former colleagues acknowledges this problem and teaches body-positive yoga with cats, which I think is pretty awesome and inclusive!

Hearing body-positive messages from PI/EAO (people of Indian/East African origins) womxn leading yoga sessions would be a welcome sight! Vegan South Asian/East African and fusion food prepared, inspired, and/or served by PI/AOs would also be a great addition at these "yoga" spaces where cafés connected to them often only serve juices and Western food. If such spaces do not want to pay homage to yoga's roots in South Asia and East Africa, then they should rename themselves as meditative or physical workout spaces so as to be politically correct and avoid recolonizing ancient traditions. (Being South Asian, I do not believe I have the authority to speak from an East African perspective, so much of my response here is from my personal South Asian perspective.)

Yoga should not be a hot commodity to generate profits for white-dominated capitalist businesses, but an accessible (both fiscally and physically), (w)holistic, and mindful consciousness-raising practice that engages in communal conversations about self-realization and wholeness with regard to its spiritual connections and indigenous roots. If yoga instructors are going to chant words from languages they're not fluent in, they need to be mindful to not butcher the pronunciations. The same goes for sacred idols and scriptures used to "decorate" so-called "yoga" studios: If the studio is not used as a spiritual space, then using spirituality as a fashion accessory is not ok. Yoga can be as personal or communal as one likes, as long as one if mindful and respectful of its pluralistic origins.

One doesn't necessarily need to pay for a class in a studio to meditate. As long as our minds and bodies are aligned, we can practice yoga and other forms of (therapeutic and spiritual) meditations from the comfort of our home or out in a public park. Given that several poses in Indian yoga are inspired by animals, such as *Marjaryasana* (cat pose) or *Adho Mukha Svanasana* (dog pose), it might be healthy to also include our animal companions in our meditation routines.

For those who are interested in learning more about yoga and avoiding cultural appropriation, Roopa Singh's *SAAPYA* (South Asian Art and Perspectives on Yoga and

America) WordPress blog is a good start.

**Deepta:** Yoga was a part of my school's curriculum in New Delhi, and I have also learned yoga under a *guru* in Bangalore. I also enjoy practicing at a studio here in the U.S. Most instructors across this continent teach *asanas* (postures); some provide a glimpse of *pranayama* (breath control) and *dhyana* (meditation). I see that many Western teachers present yoga as "a non-religious practice from the East," yet go on to chant the vedic *mantras* and *shlokas* while perfecting the various *asanas* of *surya namaskar* (salutations to the Sun deity), which are all religious practices. While anyone can practice yoga, and there are no restrictions or prerequisites based on nationality, culture, gender, race, or age, omitting or even outright denying the information about its origins deliberately sidelines Hinduism and India. Yoga itself is an intrinsic part of Hinduism. I have discussed this at length with a few yoga teachers across the East and West coasts and have mentioned the need to clearly specify this in their classes. However, I am unsure how much impact such a conversation would have since things are different in this capitalist era.

**Ankita:** Yoga for me has been more of a health and fitness regime that I have followed on and off, more in terms of deriving peace and mental toughness to be able to concentrate while surrounded by conflicting emotions and thoughts. I actively work for animal rescue and rehabilitation causes because I feel very strongly for them. While that gives me the motivation to work for them, it is a field often charged with emotion, helplessness at times, empathy, and also one that requires practical action and decision making while collaborating with people from diverse thoughts and backgrounds. That's where it helps me to stay calm and have an inner peace that translates into better work on the outside. I have mostly practiced yoga in my personal space because I prefer a conversation with my inner self. It is more meditative than exercise for me. I was introduced to yoga by people within the family, and even though I did not care much about it until exactly a decade ago, I started pursuing the meditative aspects of it soon after my first involvement in a social cause. My paternal grandfather was the first yoga enthusiast in the family. It has stayed with me since then.

Not all yoga practitioners are vegans or vegetarians. Likewise, not all yoga practitioners have spiritual or peace-promoting agendas for their practice. Sadly, yoga seems to have mostly caught on as a fitness regime for Westerners. Lavish "yoga studios" and self-styled yoga teachers are found almost everywhere nowadays. I have mostly explored yoga as a very peaceful, calm, rhythmic, and self-purifying endeavor, so I am always discouraged with seeing versions of yoga that reduce it to a fad. I sincerely hope that the distortions that yoga faces do not permanently taint the practice in the long run. We have much to lose rather than gain from the adulterated forms of capitalist-oriented yoga, and if we stand to lose its original form and structure (where its healing properties come from), we risk losing its spiritual roots.

**Laila:** Yoga is not a part of my cultural or religious heritage. Until recently, my only exposure to it was from the plethora of pictures on social media—pictures of slim, young, mostly white womxn doing yoga poses in exotic locations. This did not appeal to me at all. After reading

*Autobiography of a Yogi* by Paramahansa Yogananda a few years ago, I became interested in practicing yoga as a way of deepening my spiritual practice. My only experiences in yoga spaces, so far, have been from a Western perspective. I have attended a variety of yoga classes in London. Most of the classes have focused on the physical yoga postures. Only a few have meaningfully incorporated some of the other yoga "limbs," such as *pranayama* (conscious breathing exercises) and meditation. Most students I have encountered in the classes have also seemed more focused on perfecting the physical poses than on the wider system of yoga.

With the commercialization of yoga and the focus on the physical aspect, I can see why many feel Western yoga is a form of cultural appropriation. I only recently found out that yoga was banned in India under British colonial rule. It is understandable, then, how the ease with which some Westerners can go off to India, complete a yoga teacher training course, and make money out of teaching a spiritual practice whose history, context, and depth they may not fully understand can be upsetting to those for whom yoga is a sacred part of their culture. Some people suggest that by stripping yoga of its essence— taking it out of its original context, branding, and repackaging it for mass consumption and increased profits— is perpetuating a kind of "second colonization." I find this argument very compelling, especially when I think of all the commercialized yoga chains and studios there are now, focused purely on yoga for physical fitness. With this in mind, I am currently trying to establish my own personal practice at home. Hopefully, one day, I will find an accessible yoga space and a teacher who has a deep understanding of the history and context of yoga; one who sees yoga as a primarily spiritual practice, and understands, practices, and teaches all eight limbs of yoga (including "ethical conduct" and "nonviolence," which, for me, include veganism).

## 4. What are your impressions of most "mainstream" vegan spaces?

**Winnie:** I have had varied experiences with a lot of vegan spaces within the U.S. Even though I love being able to go to a vegan restaurant and order anything off of the menu (sans a few substitutions because of my allergies and preferences), I often fantasize about more vegan food establishments with healthier, less-processed options. I would also love seeing more vegan Punjabi (North Indian) restaurants, of which there are very few at the moment. Often, places that serve less-processed vegan foods come with a hefty price tag in the name of health. Healthy vegan foods in grocery stores, farmer's markets, food trucks, and restaurants should be accessible to those who are economically disadvantaged. Food deserts are not acceptable, and we must take collective measures to make nutritious foods accessible to all. Moreover, many places that sell vegan food often do so without regard to helping other sentient beings through voluntarism or charity: Why does part of our consumer money from each purchase at all successful vegan establishments not go to benefit nonprofit organizations and sanctuaries that are doing important work for both humans and nonhumans?

Spaces that claim to be 100% plant-based but still

serve products with honey or bee pollen, and spaces that claim to be vegetarian, but serve seafood, pose other problems. I don't support oxymoronic labels that mislead people into thinking they're buying "cruelty-free" food when in reality, they're just falling prey to marketing gimmicks. Many non-vegan places have started advertising vegan menus, but I have been disappointed to see non-vegan items on such menus at times (including one such instance at a major university's dining hall in California and another at a local Ohioan restaurant's vegan sushi menu), simply because they did not know what being "vegan" entailed (as confirmed through my conversations with their staff).

If "vegan" spaces ignore the effects of bee farming and the ethics involved around using honey and bee pollen, it complicates the situation more by blurring the boundaries between vegan and non-vegan food spaces. Furthermore, when such spaces serve food in expanded polystyrene foam containers with plastic bags and cutlery, the message of caring for other beings is lost because of the contribution of such toxic materials to ocean pollution and landfills that impact not only the health of our planet, but also that of sea life and low-income communities of color who live near such polluted areas. I have also wondered how many businesses actually source sugar that isn't processed through bone char.

In addition, vegan companies that do not use fair-trade practices or child-labor-free ingredients but benefit by selling animal liberation at the expense of other marginalized groups fail when it comes to realizing that we all share the same ecosystem and that our struggles are interconnected. Many online and offline vegan spaces are plagued with racial, classist, sizeist, and (hetero)sexist hatred, in the same way that several feminist spaces have developed blind spots to animal cruelty, environmental racism, colonialism, and (hetero)sexism. For our collective future, I envision a vegan-feminist utopia where we live healthy lives to the extent possible and where not just our shared interests but also our multitude of differences are a cause of celebration. A world in which no other animal has to suffer a lifetime of abuse, torture, and death to become a disposable resource for human greed.

**Bipasha:** I find many "mainstream" vegan spaces to be "spaces of whiteness." In other words, physical vegan spaces are often predominantly occupied by white individuals; intellectual spaces where veganism is discussed are often dominated by white voices, while the voices of people of color are talked over or simply erased. A white privileged and supremacist perspective is often perceived by those outside vegan spaces as THE perspective on veganism. This is most flagrantly demonstrated by arguments that equate the subjugation of nonhuman animals with those of humans, particularly Black people during antebellum slavery. For me, it starkly demonstrates that white supremacy and racism are a serious problem in mainstream veganism, as this type of imagery is often used without regard for descendants of slavery while the voices of these descendants – including Black vegans – are routinely drowned out by white activists. Anger at such blatant racism compels me to work toward activism that ensures the voices of vegans of color are listened to and heard. I am always relieved and reassured when I do find PoC vegan spaces. I am energized by the PoC vegan groups and sites I have been able to access and engage with on social media. I recently attended a vegan market in London, at which many of the food stalls offered vegan versions of various Indian, African, Caribbean, and Latinx dishes. It was expensive, which is an issue that needs to be desperately addressed. However, the crowd in this instance was relatively mixed compared to other vegan physical spaces, which made me feel both happy and hopeful, although I acknowledge there is still a lot of work to be done.

**Meenal:** My experiences with vegan spaces have been mixed. While veganism itself is based on justice for all nonhuman animals, I find that some vegans are still comfortable subscribing to the oppression of human animals. Sometimes, it feels like the goal is achieving a virtual badge of honor on "how much" of a vegan one is. Sadly, that attitude is highly detrimental to the cause of veganism, making it seem that veganism is merely a passing fad.

However, other vegan spaces are very progressive and inclusive. A monthly vegan potluck group I am part of here in the U.K. discusses everything related to compassionate living—from humanitarian crisis in some parts of the world, to knitting winter hats for homeless people. Most of the people in the group grew up on steaks but are now vegan, so their diet predominantly consists of "meat substitutes," and they are always interested to know about my diet as a vegan Indian. My diet helps them respond to all the "protein gibes" they tend to face—after all, we Indians have been thriving on plant-based diets for several generations, without such luxuries as plant-based "chicken" or "cheese!"

**Laila:** My main exposure to vegan spaces has been on Facebook. It is hard to make generalizations about these spaces. My impression is that many of the larger vegan Facebook pages and groups seem to be influenced by the positions of the mainstream corporate animal charities. These charities tend to promote welfare and single-issue campaigns to maintain their donor base. These campaigns are inherently speciesist and are not based on animal rights. I find they create a lot of confused positions among vegans. They also tend to perpetuate other types of oppressions, such as sexism, racism, and ableism. Even in those vegan spaces that promote animal rights, there is a lack of understanding of or interest in systemic oppressions and in connecting veganism and animal rights to other social justice issues. I often see comments like: "Stop taking the focus off animals" or "Let's keep politics out of veganism" when issues of human oppression are raised. I absolutely agree that the vegan movement should be centered on other animals, but the interconnectedness of human and animal oppressions is really hard to deny once you see it. It is essential to understand these connections if we are ever going to achieve animal liberation.

I also see mainstream vegan groups and advocates promoting sexist, ableist, or racist campaigns; they often endorse vegan celebrities who are racist, misanthropic, sexist, etc. Some also condone the use of oppressive slogans appropriated from other movements, such as "All Lives Matter." When people, often those who are directly affected by these types of behaviors, try and explain why these things are offensive, I have seen them be ignored or silenced. This reflects a certain level of privilege in vegan spaces. Our privileges allow us to ignore issues that we think don't affect us. Those in marginalized groups don't have the luxury of ignoring them. I don't think this is necessarily unique to vegan spaces, though. They reflect many of the same biases, prejudices, and ideologies as exist in wider society.

I am also part of some pro-intersectional vegan groups. I continue to learn a huge amount from the discussions in these groups. They have really helped me become aware of some of my own privileges and unconscious biases. I still have a long way to go, and I expect this will be a lifelong process, but I have noticed that, while people are regularly called out for racist, sexist, ableist, and other types of oppressive language and behaviors in these spaces, speciesism is less likely to be called out. If someone does call it out, they are often ignored or silenced. I have started to find some vegan spaces that promote total liberation where voices of those from marginalized groups are more prominent, where people understand or are willing to learn about systemic oppressions, where the connections between human and nonhuman oppressions are seen as important, and where it is understood that we need to include both humans and other animals in our anti-oppression stances. These are the spaces that need to become more representative of the vegan movement.

# 3 CONTRIBUTORS

**Authors**
Bipasha Ahmed
Michelle Carrera
Rama Ganesan
Melissa John-Charles Carrillo
Shazia Juna
Leila Kassam
Vinamarata "Winnie" Kaur
Deepta Rao
Meneka Repka
Margaret Robinson
Saryta Rodríguez
Meenal Upadhyay
Destiny Whitaker
Rayven Whitaker
Ankita Yadav

**Cover Illustrator**
Meneka Repka

**Graphic Designer**
Danae Silva Montiel

**Grant Support**
Deutscher Jugendschutz-Verband

CPSIA information can be obtained
at www.ICGtesting.com
Printed in the USA
LVHW020835160620
658145LV00016B/2001

9 780998 994611